T0057319

BOB DRURY AND TOM CLAVIN

The HEART of EVERYTHING THAT IS

The Untold Story of Red Cloud, An American Legend

Young Readers Edition
adapted by Kate Waters

Margaret K. McElderry Books
New York   London   Toronto   Sydney   New Delhi

To the children
of the Pine Ridge Indian Reservation

MARGARET K. McELDERRY BOOKS
An imprint of Simon & Schuster Children's Publishing Division
1230 Avenue of the Americas, New York, New York 10020
MARGARET K. McELDERRY BOOKS is a trademark of Simon & Schuster, Inc.
For information about special discounts for bulk purchases, please contact Simon &
Schuster Special Sales at 1-866-506-1949 or business@simonandschuster.com.
The Simon & Schuster Speakers Bureau can bring authors to your live event.
For more information or to book an event, contact the Simon & Schuster Speakers
Bureau at 1-866-248-3049 or visit our website at www.simonspeakers.com.
Book design by Vikki Sheatsley
The text for this book was set in Adobe Garamond Pro.
Manufactured in the United States of America
0217 FFG

2 4 6 8 10 9 7 5 3
Library of Congress Cataloging-in-Publication Data
Names: Drury, Bob, author. | Clavin, Tom, author.
Title: The heart of everything that is / Bob Drury and Tom Clavin.
Description: Young readers edition. | New York : Margaret K. McElderry Books,
[2017] | Includes bibliographical references and index.
Identifiers: LCCN 2016024628 | ISBN 978-1-4814-6460-4 (hardcover : alk. paper)
| ISBN 978-1-4814-6462-8 (eBook)
Subjects: LCSH: Red Cloud, 1822–1909—Juvenile literature. | Oglala Indians—
Kings and rulers—Biography—Juvenile literature. | Red Cloud's War, 1866–1867—
Juvenile literature. | Indians of North America—Wars—West (U.S.)—
Juvenile literature.
Classification: LCC E99.O3 D78 2017 | DDC 978.004/9752440092 [B]—dc23
LC record available at https://lccn.loc.gov/2016024628

It was understood, at least by the whites, that the Indians would live in the eastern section and reserve the western section, the Powder River Country, as hunting grounds open to all tribes and bands. In the center of this tract, like a glittering jewel, lay the Black Hills. Paha Sapa. The Heart of Everything That Is.   —*Red Cloud*

The HEART of EVERYTHING THAT IS

Contents

MAPS

CANADA

Lake Superior

MONTANA

NORTH DAKOTA

Chippewa

MINNESOTA

Yanktonais

WISCONSIN

Fort Snelling

Fort Howard

Hunkpapas and Blackfeet

SOUTH DAKOTA

Sioux

Eastern Sioux

Tetons

Fort Crawford

Black Hills

Miniconjous and Sans Arcs

Missouri R.

WYOMING

Fort Laramie

Niobrara R.

Yanktons

Brules

Omaha

IOWA

Sauk and Fox

Oglalas

Pawnee

Potawatomi

Cheyenne and Arapaho

NEBRASKA

Otto and Missouri

Kickapoo

ILLINOIS

Fort Kearney

Fort Leavenworth

MISSOURI

Mississippi R.

Kansas R.

COLORADO

KANSAS

Ottawa

Arkansas R.

Osage

Seneca and Shawnee

Cherokee

Fort Gibson

North Canadian R.

OKLAHOMA

Canadian R.

Creek and Seminole

Fort Smith

ARKANSAS

NEW MEXICO

Chickasaw

Choctaw

Apache

Red R.

Fort Towson

Mississippi R.

Comanche

N

TEXAS

W   E

S

LOUISIANA

The Western Tribes Before the Civil War

Contemporary state names are shown.

| 0 | 100 | 200 miles |

| 0 | 100 | 200 kilometers |

Gulf of Mexico

A Note to the Reader

You will read many names of Indian tribes and bands in the following pages, including Sioux, Pawnee, Crow, and Cheyenne. This is because there are a large number of groups of Indians, all with different languages, cultures, and customs. As the United States expanded westward in the nineteenth century, many Americans failed to see any distinction between these very different groups of peoples.

The Sioux peoples comprise two major groups of Indians: the Eastern Dakota and the Western Lakota. Among the Lakota are seven bands of Indians: Brules, Oglalas, Hunkpapas, Sans Arcs, Miniconjous, Two Kettles, and Blackfeet. These bands can be further broken into smaller groups, such as the Kiyuska and the Bad Faces.

Red Cloud was an Oglala Lakota head man of the band of Sioux called *Ite Sica,* or Bad Faces.

Prologue

1837, Nebraska

Red Cloud's heart would not fail him today.

With the news of the death of his cousin in a failed battle against the Pawnee, Red Cloud knew that today, the day Old Smoke called upon his people to retaliate, was the day he would join his first raiding party. Red Cloud had just turned sixteen. It was time to disregard his mother's pleas that he was too young. He was not. He was ready to prove himself a true warrior.

As Red Cloud painted and dusted himself and his horses in preparation for battle, a shout rose among the mothers, wives, and sisters gathered about the fighters.

"He is coming."

"Who is coming?" someone called.

"Red Cloud," called another voice, and the crowd took up a chant. "Red Cloud comes! Red Cloud comes!"

Red Cloud appeared on his spotted pony, painted and

feathered, leading a spare horse by a rope. Both his animals had ribbons entwined in their manes and tails. He was ready.

Within moments the Sioux departed. It took Red Cloud and the group ten days to reach the rough sand hills overlooking the Pawnee village.

On the eleventh day, they charged at dawn. The roaring sound of battle began as elk-bone whistles shrieked and high-pitched war whoops cut the air. Red Cloud steered his horse through the Pawnee camp, ducking as arrows and musket balls ripped through the blankets and skins hanging from the entrances to the earthen Pawnee lodges.

He was right. His heart would not fail him that day. The fierce fighting between the tribes ended, and when the Sioux returned home, four warriors paraded from lodge to lodge, lifting Pawnee scalps high on their spears in celebration. One of the four was Red Cloud. On his first raiding party, barely sixteen years old, he had proved himself worthy as a warrior. He had made his first kill.

PART ONE

Red Cloud

I hope the Great Heavenly Father, who will look down upon us, will give all the tribes his blessing, that we may go forth in peace and live in peace all our days, and that He will look down upon our children and finally lift us above this earth.   —*Red Cloud*

Early Life

One quiet night on the plains of Nebraska, a glowing red meteor raced across the sky. Below it, a band of Brule Lakota Indians camped. Those who saw the meteor knew it was a sign of some kind—whether it was good or bad would be determined in the future. A few days later at the edge of the camp, a woman named Walks as She Thinks spread a brushed deerskin blanket over a bed of sand on the banks of Blue Water Creek and gave birth to her first son.

When the infant's father, Lone Man, announced to the band that he had named the boy after the strange meteorological occurrence to appease the Great Spirit, the Brules agreed that he had done a wise thing.

This is how the child came to be called *Makhpiya-luta,* or Red Cloud.

When Red Cloud was only four years old, his father, Lone Man, died because of his addiction to what the white man called whiskey. In reality, the drink, sold or traded to the Indians, was a shuddering mixture of diluted alcohol, molasses, tobacco juice, and crushed red pepper. Native Americans of the eighteenth and nineteenth centuries had no more immunity to alcohol than to smallpox.

Lone Man's death left a lasting impression. Red Cloud hated the distilled *mini wakan*—"the water that makes men crazy"—for the rest of his life.

After Lone Man's death Red Cloud's mother, Walks as She Thinks, left the Brule camp and took him, his younger brother, Big Spider, and an infant sister back to her original Oglala Lakota band, which was led by Old Smoke. Old Smoke recognized her as a "sister," a term that meant that she was either his true sibling or a close cousin with the same status as a sister. Although Old Smoke was by then in his early fifties, he was still a vibrant war leader; he had been a head man for close to two decades, and his band was the largest, strongest, and most influential of all the Oglala tribes, if not of the Sioux nation.

The Sioux instilled in their children a respect for reserve and poise. Another uncle, a warrior named White Hawk, taught the young Red Cloud to control what he called the boy's "unusually headstrong impulses." In the future, these impulses would help to establish Red Cloud's reputation for vicious behavior in war.

White Hawk was also responsible, along with Walks as She Thinks, for the child's education. They interpreted for him the messages to be found in every birdsong and the track of every animal, the significance of the eagle feather in a war bonnet, and the natural history of the Sioux. By the age of six, Red Cloud was sitting at council fires with his elders.

When Red Cloud was thirteen years old, he watched Old Smoke suppress his own cousin Bull Bear's attempt to take control of the band. Bull Bear—a sour man, with a face like a clenched fist—had strength in numbers. But Old Smoke had the loyalty of his brother White Hawk's less numerous but better-armed *akicita,* the tribe's select male society of warriors and marshals.

In the end, Bull Bear's followers thought better of challenging them. Under Lakota custom and with White Hawk's braves at his back, Old Smoke could have confiscated Bull Bear's horses and women as punishment for his behavior. Instead, he banished Bull Bear and his followers, greatly weakening his own band in the process.

Humiliated, Bull Bear threw dust in Old Smoke's face before riding out of camp. It was an act of disrespect Red Cloud never forgot and it is the likely reason Old Smoke's band got a new name. Their sullen, fierce reaction to the insult may be why they became known as the *Ite Sica,* or Bad Faces.

The Lakota rarely stayed in any one location, following the game along rivers that acted as natural highways through the western plains, seeking fresh pasturage for their expanding herds of ponies, and camping along trails in places that had acquired mystical significance. These journeys pushed the tribe farther and farther west and southwest out of South Dakota.

Life on the lush prairie offered Indian men and boys

plenty of opportunity for self-reflection and long, thoughtful conversations deep into the night as the camp's women did most of the hard work. Red Cloud had ample time to absorb his uncles' wisdom and insights regarding the Sioux philosophy of existence.

The Sioux regarded the universe as a living and breathing—if mysterious—being. And though they recognized the passage of time as measured by the predictable movements of the sun, the moon, and the stars, to their eyes mankind was but a flickering flame in a strong wind. Their concepts of past, present, and future were blurred so that all three existed simultaneously, on separate planes.

Americans steeped in Christian culture and Victorian science failed to understand this Indian approach to life. They often threw up their hands and resorted to the cliché of Indian spirituality as a blend of ignorance and superstition. Ignorance of Indian ways also contributed greatly to the white man's description of Indians as untamed, savage, wild people lacking personal discipline. There was, however, a precise structure supporting Sioux religious beliefs, even if it remained largely unrecognizable to outsiders.

Sioux religious philosophy flowed from their recognition of what the famous Oglala holy man Black Elk described as the "Sacred Hoop" of life. That hoop consists of a series of concentric circles, divine rings, the smallest of which surrounds one's immediate family. The hoops expand outward, growing ever larger to include extended households, bands, tribes, entire peoples, the earth and all its living things, and finally the universe, *Wakan Tanka*.

A Lakota camp in South Dakota. Tepees were made of buffalo hide
and could be put up and taken down in minutes.
Photo by John C. H. Grabill, c. 1891, Library of Congress

American bison. Some have begun to shed their winter coats.
Photo by Pelck's Scenic & Art Studio, c. 1906, Library of Congress

So while whites viewed animals in terms of their usefulness as food or workers, the Sioux saw them as nearly equal and as feeling beings. Red Cloud learned from his elders, for instance, that running down a single buffalo that had escaped from one of their hunts was a question not of greed but of necessity, done so the beast would not warn others of its kind away. This was the sort of knowledge and wisdom that dominated conversation in each tepee, and in this regard Red Cloud was fortunate to have Old Smoke as a kinsman.

Old Smoke honored Red Cloud as if he were a son. He invited Red Cloud to occupy the *catku,* a section of the Sioux tepee opposite the entrance, and where the head of the family slept, sat, and discussed important matters. While the women and infants generally lived on the other side of the fire, closer to the tepee's entrance, the eldest son sat with his father in the *catku* until about the age of six, learning and observing. It was in Old Smoke's *catku* that Red Cloud absorbed his first life lessons.

Old Smoke's band of Sioux probably comprised a dozen or so extended families, which, in the spirit of the Sacred Hoop, raised their children collectively. Whites were later shocked by how the Sioux treated their children, especially their boys. Young males were continually showered with love, did nothing but play games, and were rarely punished.

The Sioux were equally appalled when they saw white fathers on the settler trails beating their children to instill discipline. All the games Lakota boys played were intended to hone their tracking, hunting, and fighting skills. Achieving excellence in these areas was the only means of advancement in Sioux society.

By the age of three or four, for instance, boys would be gathered in packs, presented with toy arrows and spears, and told to pick out an object—a rock, a tree—at a short distance and aim for it. The boy who came closest kept all the "weapons." As the boys grew, so did the distance from the targets, until at around the age of twelve they were given otter- or dog-skin quivers to hold their arrows and real bows constructed of strong, dried sage that could propel either stone or iron-tipped arrows completely through a buffalo, or a man.

Boys and young braves loved pastimes involving clubs, sticks, and rocks that often knocked them silly. A version of "king of the hill" was popular—with the "attackers" given shortened lances to fight against the "king." There was one major difference from the game as we know it: Sioux boys played at night, when stealth was crucial.

Red Cloud, blessed with strength and coordination well beyond those of his contemporaries, excelled in these competitions. Perhaps because he was a child whose father had died not in battle or on the hunt but from whiskey, he stood just outside the ring of light thrown by the lodge fires of boys with important fathers. It was always Red Cloud who hit hardest with the lance during king of the hill, or laughed loudest while confiscating the other boys' toy weapons. Such was his temper that he was sometimes warned by his uncles to curb his cruel streak.

As soon as a Sioux boy was capable of straddling a pony,

his father, an older brother, or—as in Red Cloud's case—an uncle would present him with a colt and its tack. He was instructed in the colt's care and feeding, and it was made clear to him that the precious horse was now his responsibility. Preteens learned basic horsemanship through pony races, when they gripped tight the reins of the 850-pound animals and tried not to bounce off the rough saddles.

As they grew older, one of their most important chores was caring for the family's herd. When a family was too poor to furnish a son with his own horse, his peers lent him a colt to break. This ensured that each male member of the band grew up with a thorough knowledge of horsemanship. The older the boys became, the more closely their horse games simulated raids and buffalo hunts. Red Cloud took naturally to this horse culture, and especially to the hunt.

The advantages the horse provided the Sioux in both hunting and warfare cannot be overstated. Hunting parties on fast Indian ponies could track, out-gallop, and kill buffalo in ways never before possible. Although the bands still occasionally drove an entire herd over a cliff when the opportunity presented itself, gone were the days when a party of hunters camouflaged in wolf skins were forced on their bellies to approach a single bull or cow, remove it from the herd, and bring it down with a volley of arrows. Now a solitary mounted brave, his pony stretched out and galloping low, could do the work of a half-dozen men.

How the Sioux distributed the buffalo parts also changed with the coming of the horse. Hunting, particularly cliff-driving, had once been a group effort on foot. Now the killer of a slain beast could be identified by the distinctive designs and fletching of the arrows that brought the animal down. Although the meat was still shared among the band, the hides were awarded to the household of the arrows' owners, and this too marked a subtle change in tribal hierarchy.

With individual hunters rewarded, competitive boys became even more anxious to prove themselves. By the time Sioux boys reached their early teens, the most skilled of them could bury two dozen arrows into a buffalo's short ribs with deadly accuracy in the time it took an American to fire and reload his musket. One frontiersman watched an exhibition put on by Lakota boys and noted, "They could hit a button, pencil, or any small article at about thirty yards." Red Cloud developed this skill.

Early white observers of a Sioux buffalo chase described it as barely controlled chaos, with braves even knocking one another out of the saddle. These watchers saw this as just another example of the Indians' lack of discipline. Whites had not been trained to detect the hunt's formal structure. The action was aggressively policed by *akicita* outriders, who would bring down any brave who got out ahead of the advancing line of attackers and spooked a herd prematurely. In later years, Indians who had grown up riding with Red Cloud said there was nothing in life he enjoyed so much as the spirit and excitement of the buffalo run.

Where the buffalo ranged, Old Smoke and his band followed, usually breaking and making new summer camps at least once a week in order to find fresh pasturage. In his autobiography, Red Cloud had little to report about his early youth. Perhaps he did not think his life important until he became a hunter and warrior.

Old Smoke's band would have roamed through all the major river valleys, from the Republican in the south to the Yellowstone in the north to the Missouri in the east, and would have been familiar with Nebraska's Sand Hills, the Black Hills straddling what is today's South Dakota–Wyoming border, and even the Laramie Range on the eastern face of the Rockies.

Red Cloud would have been taught to recognize plants such as the special riverbank sage that warded off evil spirits, heed signs that buffalo were near, and differentiate scat from a grizzly with a belly full of elk from the scat of a hungry bear that might be on the prowl for a Lakota horse. Becoming one with his physical environment was as natural a part of an Indian child's education as learning to read and write was to an American one.

Becoming a Warrior

It was impossible to become a Sioux leader without also being a distinguished warrior, and no one was more prepared than Red Cloud. "When I was young among our nation, I was poor," he once said. "But from the wars with one nation or another, I raised myself to be a chief."

Red Cloud was about sixteen years old when he joined his first raiding party. He had always, if reluctantly, obeyed the pleas of his mother when she argued that he was too young to take part in these raids. A Sioux woman could not be a chief, but Walks as She Thinks did speak with some authority because of her brothers' standing.

Still, the respect afforded Old Smoke and White Hawk could not change the fact that Red Cloud's absence from the war parties was beginning to be remarked on. And so Red Cloud, almost at war-party age, joined his fellow warriors on a raid against the Pawnee. It was during this raid that he made his first kill.

When he returned to his tribe after the raid, Red Cloud's mother took the reins of his horse's bridle and led him to his lodge. When he and Walks as She Thinks reached their tepee, the boy dismounted, entered, put away his weapons, and waited. Soon enough, a young female cousin called at the entrance. She beckoned him to his uncle's lodge. Red Cloud rose, wrapped himself in a blanket, and strode through the camp. Veteran braves grunted and yipped in approval, and young women stole peeks at the conquering hero.

When he reached Old Smoke's tepee, he was fed a delicious meal and prompted to recount his performance, particularly his scalp-taking. He would tell the story many times that day, including during his first appearance in the warrior lodge, the village's largest, where men spun tales of battle so that the narratives might be remembered and become public property. Meanwhile, the fires in the tepees of the men who had not returned were doused, and in the surrounding hills the wails of their women echoed for hours as they cut their hair and flesh in mourning rituals, some even chopping off fingers.

The next morning, amid more feasting, a tall medicine pole was erected in the center of the camp, and at dusk, ceremonial fires were lit in a circle around it. When the sun set, a drumbeat announced the victory dance. For the next two days and nights, the warriors danced without stopping; should one drop from exhaustion, another would take his place. Those like Red Cloud who had killed an enemy used a dye that was made from mineral deposits to paint themselves black from head to toe to appear frightening.

The most important ceremony was saved for the end of the dance. It was then that the distribution of the Pawnee horses took place. Most were kept by their captors, but some were given to the tribe's old, poor, and infirm. That day, Red Cloud proudly gave away the one pony he had captured, learning a great lesson. For the first time, someone was in his debt.

After his first killing, Red Cloud noted another important lesson—warriors who had physically struck an enemy without killing him, or "counted coup," were accorded the tribe's highest respect, more so than those who had taken scalps. Among the western tribes it was understood that the greatest courage was displayed by coming close enough to smell a man's hot breath while striking, or "quirting," him and allowing him to live. The theory was that in so doing, a brave took a greater chance of being killed himself.

Though just a teenager, Red Cloud was starting to understand how the ancient customs could be used, even by a fatherless boy, to gain power. It was the opening of Red Cloud's strategic and tactical mind, and he stored this knowledge for use during the rest of his life.

Counting Coup

It was the winter after Red Cloud's first kill, and Old Smoke's Bad Faces had staked camp in a small cottonwood valley close to where the Laramie River flows into the North Platte River near the Nebraska-Wyoming border. It had been an unusually severe March. Under the cover of a blizzard, a raiding party of fourteen Crows, on foot and far from their Montana homeland, had closed to within about ten miles of the Sioux pony herd when they were spotted by a lone Oglala brave out hunting deer.

The mounted Sioux hunter raced back to camp, and that night a party of fifty to sixty braves, including Red Cloud, rode out to ambush the Crows. They circled behind them, and by dawn they had the raiders trapped near the mouth of a tight canyon and unaware of their predicament. The Sioux charged, their gunshots and battle cries echoing off the canyon's granite walls.

The Crows, weak from their trek and caught completely

by surprise, recognized that they were too outnumbered to survive. They knelt in the snow, pulled their blankets over their heads, and sang their death songs. Red Cloud, the first of the attackers to reach them, drew his bow, slowed his horse, and struck three of the Crows in the back of the head. He then rode off a bit and turned to watch his tribesmen annihilate the intruders.

The victory banquet that night was a muted affair. The Bad Faces well understood that little glory had been achieved by massacring enemies who refused to fight back. Only one young brave was singled out to be celebrated, for he had struck the Crows while they were still alive and armed. As Red Cloud had anticipated, his stature within the tribe soared that night. He was a quick learner and, the Crow coup notwithstanding, a quicker killer.

In later years, when old Sioux who had ridden with Red Cloud reminisced, they often recalled three traits the young brave always exhibited. The first, surprisingly, was his grace. He rode, walked, and stalked like a panther, making only necessary movements. The second was his brutality; he was like flint, they said—hard and easily sparked. On one occasion he killed a Crow boy who was guarding a herd of ponies, and the next day he waited in ambush for the pursuing Crow chief, the boy's father, in order to kill him, too. Another time, he took obvious joy in jumping into a river to save a floundering Ute from drowning, only to drag him up onto the bank, knife him to death, and scalp him. The third trait was his arrogance, essential to any Sioux leader and demonstrated by a famous story about the one and only time he allowed a captured enemy to live.

It occurred while Red Cloud was leading a horse raid against the Crows. Before reaching their camp, he and his braves ambushed a small party of Blackfeet who had arrived first. As the Blackfeet were escaping with a herd of stolen mustangs, the Oglalas captured one brave. They brought him to Red Cloud, who told the man that if he could withstand what would come next without uttering a single sound, he would live to see his family again.

Red Cloud then handed his knife to his best friend, a Lakota brave named White Horse, who had recently lost a cousin in battle. He told White Horse to scalp the man alive. Two Lakota took hold of the Blackfoot's arms as Red Cloud stood before him, his heavy war club raised. White Horse walked behind the Blackfoot, grabbed his braid, and took the scalp at its roots. The Indian, his body trembling, blood running down his face, never made a noise.

True to his word, Red Cloud told him to return to his village and tell his people that it was the Lakota warrior Red Cloud who had done this to him. Red Cloud had guessed that the Blackfoot would withstand the agony in silence, and as much as he coveted an enemy's scalp, it was more important at this stage that rival tribes learned, and feared, his name.

On another occasion, the teenage Red Cloud joined a large party on a raid into Crow lands. Resting by day and riding by night, and traveling only through rugged ravines and over wooded creek bottoms that provided cover in enemy

American artist George Catlin spent many years visiting American Indian villages. He made this sketch of a Sioux village in 1850. You can see tepees, meat drying on racks, and people stretching a hide on the ground. *Rare Book Division, the New York Public Library*

territory, the Sioux took twice the usual time to cover the distance.

Red Cloud, impatient with the cautious pace set by the expedition's leaders—two prominent warriors named Old Man Afraid of His Horses and Brave Bear—suggested that they were in fact much closer to the Crow encampment than they realized. The two elder men disagreed, and Red Cloud did not argue. He was learning to control his temper, to refrain from blurting out an insult that might make him an enemy for life. Instead, he waited for his tribesmen to retire for a rare night's rest, then put on a thick pair of moccasins and sneaked away on foot with a trusted friend.

The two walked for miles before they heard a faint sound, perhaps a horse's whinny. They settled on a ridgeline to await the dawn. At the first streaks of light in the east, they saw below them a herd of fifty Crow mustangs quietly feeding on a small, grassy plateau. The remuda was guarded by a lone sentry who was sleeping with his back against a tree. There was no Crow village in sight. They crawled down to the herd, caught two fine horses, and mounted.

Red Cloud signaled to his friend to lead the small herd in the direction of the Bad Faces camp, and rode his own horse toward the sleeping Crow. When he was only a few yards from the sentry, he raised his war club and broke into a gallop. The horse's pounding hooves awakened the Crow, who ducked seconds before Red Cloud's club slammed into the tree at the spot where the man's head had been.

The terrified Crow took off at a sprint. Red Cloud, still mounted, calmly retrieved an arrow from his quiver, nocked it, and sent it into the man's back. He trotted up to the writhing body, dismounted, grabbed the victim's own knife from his belt, and killed him before scalping him.

The ride back to the Sioux camp was far from triumphant. Red Cloud warned his companion that they might be in trouble and were likely to be subjected to the whipping that usually was the punishment for a disobedient warrior. When they were met on the trail by the Lakota raiding party, several *akicita* indeed charged them, with riding whips, called quirts, raised.

But at commands from Brave Bear and Old Man Afraid of His Horses, they halted, and Red Cloud was ordered to state his case. He related his adventure and showed them the scalp. He said that he would never have risked his tribesmen's lives if the Crow horses had been tied up near an enemy camp where warning cries could have been raised. He added that judging by the horse tracks he had seen, he could indicate where the Crows kept an even larger herd. The two elders sent Red Cloud and his friend back to the temporary camp, deciding to reserve judgment, and punishment, until they followed up on this intelligence.

The next day, when the party returned with another 250 stolen mustangs that had been captured in a dawn raid on the Crow village—located exactly where Red Cloud had guessed—Red Cloud was forgiven. He was also awarded half of the fifty horses he had taken. His fellow warriors took approving note. Red Cloud was now a rich man.

The Sun Dance

By the time Red Cloud reached his late teens, he had established his fighting qualities: reckless bravery, stealth, and strength. He once single-handedly killed four Pawnee in battle, and his massacres of men and boys—Arikara, Snakes, Gros Ventres, and Crows—were becoming legendary. He was a living embodiment of the belief that war is the best teacher of war; in his case, too much was never enough.

As a striving young brave, he did not spare himself the self-inflicted pain common in Sioux warrior culture. There were numerous self-torture and purification rites that Lakota fighting men undertook, but none was as fearsome as the annual Sun Dance ceremony.

The Sun Dance ceremony lasted two weeks and was usually held in July before the late-summer raiding season. It is likely that Red Cloud performed his own Sun Dance purification when he was a teenager. Sioux men (and, in a few rare cases, women) believed that only by subjecting the body to excruciating physical suffering could an individual release the spirit imprisoned in the flesh and come to understand the true meaning of life.

This ritual was the key, the Sioux believed, to gaining a physical edge, to avoiding bad luck and illness, and to ensuring success during the hunt and in battle. Warriors like Red Cloud felt that the Sun Dance ceremony made them much harder to kill. The rituals of the Sun Dance were the price paid by those who hoped to become tribal leaders.

The Sun Dance was always voluntary, and whenever possible it was performed in the shadow of *Mato Paha:* Bear Butte, the majestic 1,200-foot mountain in present-day western South Dakota, long revered as a holy place by both the Lakota and the Cheyenne. The ceremony was initiated by a warrior through a simple vow to a celestial god to exchange his suffering for heavenly protection.

A young Lakota, typically in his late teens or early twenties, would approach older men who had undergone the ordeal to help guide him through it. The dance was generally held in public, sometimes in a specific lodge set up for the occasion, but more often in the center of the village. There a painted pole made from the trunk of a forked cottonwood, representing the Tree of Life, was set in the earth.

The dancer believed that this symbolic tree connected him to his creator. The older men would pierce either side of the Sun Dancer's chest, and sometimes the back flesh near the shoulder blades, and push slivers of wood through the cuts. Then they looped rawhide strips over the exposed ends

Surrounded by elders and women, young warriors gather to take part in a Sun Dance. *Library of Congress*

Bear Butte Mountain rises above the South Dakota plains. Fort Meade was a cavalry fort with barracks and stables.
Photo by John C. H. Grabill, c. 1888, Library of Congress

of the wooden pieces and tied the free ends of the lines to the center pole. In extreme cases, heavy buffalo skulls would be hung from the incisions in the brave's back.

As medicine men uttered prayers and female relatives trilled and wailed to a steady drumbeat, the Sun Dancer whirled around the pole, going through a series of ancient dance steps, for twenty-four hours. The ceremony ended in one of two ways. Either the dancer would fling himself backward from the pole, ripping his own flesh, or his older mentors would seize him and yank him back hard. In either instance the result was the same. The slivers would burst from his chest and back, and the ragged bits of flesh would be trimmed away with a ceremonial knife and laid at the foot of the pole as an offering to the sun.

For Red Cloud, the Sun Dance had multiple purposes. The most fundamental was that as a Sioux warrior he needed all the celestial help he could get. But he also saw the sacrifice as another rung on the ladder to tribal acceptance and prominence. Red Cloud was a skilled fighter, and he was also showing his resourcefulness. The young brave may have gone out of his way to demonstrate it to his peers as a sign that he was capable of one day becoming their chief.

A Sign of
Prominence

When Red Cloud was a teenager, his uncle White Hawk, the Bad Faces' *blotahunka,* commander of the tribe's *akicita,* was killed—some say by the bitter Bull Bear—and his charismatic young nephew inherited the bleached white bull-hide buffalo shield signifying his rank.

Red Cloud now commanded a select society responsible for not only protecting the band from outside enemies but acting as a sort of police force to maintain tribal discipline during buffalo hunts and amid the controlled chaos when the village moved from one pasturage to another.

One autumn, while the band was camped in a thicket, Red Cloud led a party of about forty hunters out onto the buffalo grass to stock their winter larders. These hunts could be monthlong affairs, with the Indians moving every two or three days from one temporary campsite to the next as they followed the herd and loaded their packhorses with piles of hides and dried meat. On this occasion they were joined by

Strips of buffalo meat were hung over poles to dry. The meat would last through the winter when hunting was difficult.
Photo by Edward S. Curtis, 1908, Library of Congress

a party of Cheyenne, who had staked their own winter camp about a mile away.

The next day, a sobbing Bad Face woman came to Red Cloud to tell him that while gathering water, she had been molested by a Cheyenne brave. Red Cloud questioned her, realized he knew who the man was, and gathered seven of his *akicita* to ride to the Cheyenne village. Aside from his gun, bow, and quiver of arrows, he also carried an old Spanish saber.

On reaching the village, he ordered his men to form a circle around the Cheyenne brave's lodge, stepped inside alone, and began to club the man with the flat of the steel blade. The Cheyenne's howls and yelps, not to mention the presence of "foreign" warriors in the camp, naturally attracted attention. Soon a large group of armed Cheyenne had surrounded the Sioux. The *akicita* signed that Red Cloud was inside righting a wrong, and that all should stand back. Astonishingly, the Cheyenne obeyed.

Soon enough, the cries from the tepee turned to whimpers, and Red Cloud stepped out. He wordlessly signaled his men to mount and led them out of the camp at a gallop.

This episode was extraordinary on several levels. As a general rule at the time, when Indians were angry enough to fight, they were angry enough to kill. Fights between individuals from separate tribes were rare. The fact that Red Cloud, of all people, had left the Cheyenne man alive seemed to run against the grain of his warrior's nature.

But what is almost beyond comprehension is the fact that a band of Cheyenne, known for their courage as well as for their hair-trigger tempers, did not retaliate when a small party of Sioux rode into their camp and formed a human chain around one of their lodges while, inside, their tribesman was beaten to a bloody pulp.

The only explanation is that the man executing the rough justice was Red Cloud, whose fame had now spread throughout the Powder River Basin and beyond.

6

Showdown
with Bull Bear

Red Cloud was a young man in his early twenties when everything changed for him. The Bad Faces had staked winter lodges on the Laramie plain along Chugwater Creek, and camping not far off was Old Smoke's antagonist, Bull Bear, and his band of Kiyuska.

Bull Bear's aggressive reputation had attracted many warriors—more than were drawn to any other band—and a council of Oglala elders had selected him as a sort of head man for the entire tribe. Although the electors respected Old Smoke, they were hesitant to bestow such an honor on a man who was now in his sixties and who had changed physically and mentally.

There was also an ugly memory to consider.

Some years back, white traders near Fort Laramie, the American trading post situated in today's southeastern Wyoming, had begun to treat Old Smoke as the "chief" of the Oglalas. This annoyed Bull Bear, and he had ridden up to Old Smoke's tepee in the Bad Face camp and challenged him to a fight. When Old Smoke failed to come out of his lodge and meet him, Bull Bear slit the throat of the "chief's" favorite horse. None of this sat well with Red Cloud. But given Sioux principles and his own lack of stature at the time, there was little Red Cloud could do about it. Undoubtedly, the elders took this into account when they named Bull Bear as their leader.

Now, before settling down for that winter of 1841–42, Red Cloud led a small party on one last autumn raid into Ute country in present-day Utah and western Colorado. Upon his return to the camp on Chugwater Creek—leading a string of stolen ponies, and with a Ute scalp fixed to his lance—he learned that in his absence, a Bad Face brave had run off with a Kiyuska girl.

The girl's father, an ally of Bull Bear's, was demanding payback from the Bad Faces. Red Cloud must have thought this rich. "Stealing" a woman was a rather mundane fact of life among the Lakota—particularly if the woman was not opposed to being "stolen," as seemed to be the case here.

Nevertheless, the Kiyuska were not in the habit of letting go of what they thought an insult, and Bull Bear was certain to view any wrongdoing, however minor, as an attack on his authority. Red Cloud was told that Bull Bear was personally plotting a showdown.

In theory, the same Lakota council of elders who had chosen Bull Bear as head man would rule on disputes such as this. The Kiyuska leader, however, was not a man to stand on ceremony. A head man depended on loyal warriors, and Bull

Bear had formed blood ties to numerous Oglala braves since his split with Old Smoke. Over time, he had also developed a dangerous taste for the white man's alcohol.

After draining several jugs of *mini wakan,* Bull Bear and his braves rode to the Bad Faces camp. The first person they encountered was the father of the brave who had run off with the Kiyuska girl. The circumstances are unclear, but the man may have gone out to meet Bull Bear specifically to make amends for his son's actions. Bull Bear shot him dead.

At the report of the rifle, a dozen Bad Faces, including Red Cloud, poured from the warriors' lodge. Rifle volleys and arrows were exchanged, and one shot grazed Bull Bear's leg, knocking him from his saddle. As he sat dazed on the ground, half drunk, blood seeping from his thigh, Red Cloud rushed to him. He shouted, "You are the cause of this!" and then hefted a rifle and shot him.

Bull Bear died instantly. After the gun smoke cleared, the Oglala elders once again found themselves trying to maintain a fragile peace between the Bad Faces and Kiyuska. In the end, the fact that the Kiyuska remained the more numerous tribe swung the selection, and the council elected Bull Bear's son, who was also named Bull Bear but now took the name Whirlwind, to succeed his father as head man.

It was a turning point in Sioux history. Though Whirlwind was the chosen head man, it was evident to all that Red Cloud, barely out of his teens, had become the de facto warrior chief of the Oglala tribe—and, by extension, of the Lakota nation.

. . .

The four pillars of Sioux leadership—acknowledged by the tribe to this day—are bravery, fortitude, generosity, and wisdom. Time and again Red Cloud exhibited each of these. Yet, traditionally, the Lakota also considered lesser factors when weighing the attributes of an aspiring head man.

One was the support of important religious medicine men. Red Cloud was a crafty enough politician to recognize this, and his gifts of horses to the shamans and vision seekers, as well as the lavish piles of meat his hunting forays provided to the entire band—with holy men usually receiving the choicest cuts—were more than enough to sway opinion.

The second factor was a trickier business. It involved the membership of a man's father in important fraternal societies. Among the Oglalas, even Red Cloud's strong maternal bloodline could not completely erase the memory of his alcoholic Brule father. He would always lack the prestige of a head man like Whirlwind, son of Bull Bear.

Red Cloud faced and accepted this prejudice while doing his best to overcome it. He joined numerous warrior societies, and went out of his way to aid the weak, the poor, and the old among his band in particular and the tribe in general. Around 1850, as he turned twenty-nine, he also calculated the advantage of marrying into the right family in order to seal power alliances.

A Sioux man could take as many wives as he could afford—the bride price always involved the transfer of property, usually horses. Aside from his Brule lineage, Red Cloud's desirability as a son-in-law was apparent, and the parents of the tribe's most eligible maidens knew it. Thus, marriage

Saliva, an Oglala Sioux priest, wearing a buffalo robe and holding a pipe. *Photo by Edward S. Curtis, 1907, Library of Congress*

happened. Red Cloud married Pretty Owl, the daughter of an influential subchief, securing his status in his tribe. He, unlike most others, claimed to have been monogamous for the rest of his life.

He was fortunate in another matter: he was born at the right moment in Sioux history. And though he was destined to become more feared than his contemporaries Sitting Bull and Crazy Horse, his story has been long forgotten by conventional American history. His beginnings gave some indication of his prowess as a warrior. From there, his journey led to his role as a respected, brave chief of the Lakota nation.

PART TWO

The White Man

The white man made me a lot of promises, and they only kept one. They promised to take my land, and they took it.

—*Red Cloud*

Intruders from the East

Fort William, situated in southeastern Wyoming, was the only American trading post west of the Missouri River in the 1830s. Money could be made selling buffalo robes in the East, and the men who ran Fort William—Robert Campbell and his partner, William Sublette—did good business, especially with the Lakota for buffalo cow hides.

A fifteen-foot wall of cottonwood logs and a cannon mounted in a blockhouse over the front gate protected Fort William. It became a regular winter transit point for Indians roaming across the Powder River Country. White–Indian interactions were generally peaceable. Given their isolation and small numbers, Campbell and Sublette and the few teamsters they employed were wise to keep relations calm.

The Indians, meanwhile, not only wanted and needed the supplies Campbell imported, but saw no glory to be gained by wiping the white men out. The Lakota, in any case, were busy expanding their territory, raiding and fighting the Crows, Ute, Pawnee, and Kiowa at every opportunity.

Pierre Chouteau of the St. Louis Missouri Fur Company purchased Fort William, and in 1841, renamed Fort William as Fort John and expanded the old post. A fifteen-foot adobe wall went up around the half-acre courtyard, living quarters, and warehouses, and he added a crude blacksmith's shop. Two cannon towers, called bastions, were positioned on opposite corners of the stockade. A set of large double gates made the structure look threatening.

One day, a wagon train known as the Bidwell-Bartleson caravan, guided by mountain man Thomas Fitzpatrick, stopped at Fort John to resupply before heading to California. Though it may have been small, with only eighty travelers, its importance was not.

The trails opened by the first frontier explorers in the 1820s and 1830s had initially drawn scientists, missionaries, and even wealthy sportsmen to the pristine territory on the far side of the Missouri River. On their return to the East, these men spun beautiful tales about the glories of the new Eden beyond the river. Their stories were lapped up by newspaper reporters.

In 1846, one New York City paper, noting the arrival in Manhattan of two British aristocrats recently returned from an "extended buffalo-hunting tour in Oregon and the Wild West," used the terms "wonders," "agreeable," "grand," "glowing," and "magnificent" in one paragraph alone to describe the wild country. "The fisheries are spoken of as the best in

In the mid-1800s the trading post was where both Indians and settlers stocked up on supplies. *By Karl Bodmer, [between 1832 and 1843], Library of Congress*

Sport hunters pose with a buffalo carcass. This photo was taken in 1904. *Library of Congress*

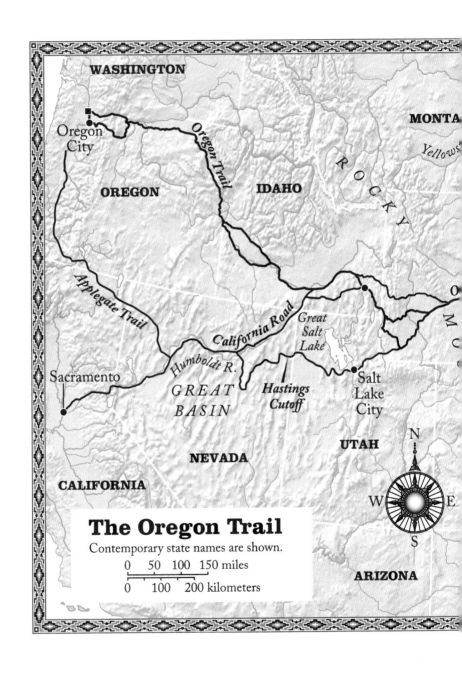

WASHINGTON

Oregon City

OREGON

Oregon Trail

IDAHO

ROCKY

MONTA

Yellows*

Applegate Trail

California Road

Great Salt Lake

Humboldt R.

GREAT BASIN

Hastings Cutoff

Salt Lake City

Sacramento

UTAH

M U

NEVADA

CALIFORNIA

N

W   E

S

ARIZONA

The Oregon Trail

Contemporary state names are shown.

| 0 | 50 | 100 | 150 miles |

| 0 | 100 | 200 kilometers |

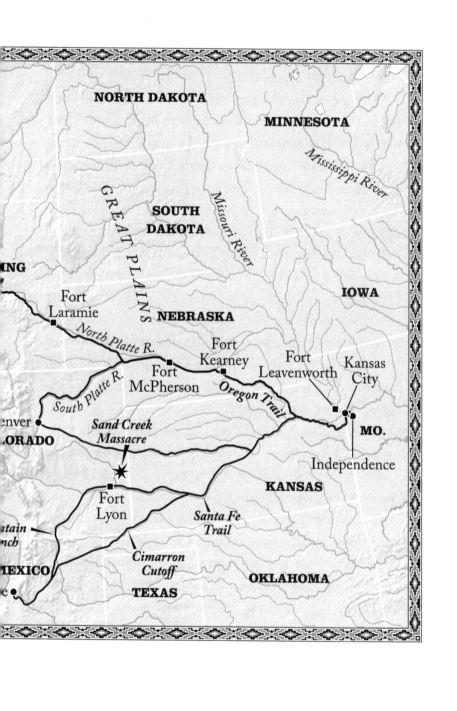

the country," the article concluded, "and only equalled by the rare facilities for agriculture."

This piqued the imagination of thousands of small farmers and city dwellers who were eager to begin a new life in paradise. A family or its extended clan just needed to scrape together the $400 required to outfit a wagon with stock and provisions. Many could. The general course of the Oregon Trail, a new wagon road branching off from the older, more established Santa Fe Trail in Kansas, had been mapped and described by the explorer John Frémont in 1842. The rutted route worked its way northwest over the Rockies at the South Pass, and it soon surpassed the Santa Fe Trail as a symbol of the nation's expansion.

For most of the 1840s, the High Plains tribes remained too busy warring with one another to bother with the small caravans of covered wagons that snaked across the plains pulled by oxen and by mules.

On the occasions when the wagons did arouse Indians' curiosity, their owners could usually pass freely after offering a small payment of coffee or refined sugar, which the Indians considered a particular delicacy.

Still, to the Sioux in particular, the white travelers were an odd lot. In his later years, Red Cloud recalled watching in puzzlement as the ignorant pioneers—overconfident if under-outfitted and pathetically unprepared for the harsh, treeless prairie—burned expensive steamer trunks, furniture, and even the occasional pipe organ for cook fires. The settlers littered the wheatgrass and fox sedge with discarded goose-feather mattresses, grandfather clocks, and portable sawmills in belated attempts to lighten the load on axles made from young, green wood that too often snapped hauling such extravagances.

What had begun as a trickle turned into a wave of home-steaders bound for Oregon's lush Willamette River Valley, miners bound for the goldfields of California, and Mormons bound for the Salt Lake country. The first Mormon wagon train moved up the Platte River in the spring of 1847 on the Mormon Trail, a route that merged with the Oregon Trail at Fort John before crossing the mountains.

The Lakota, in particular the Oglalas, were initially help-less in the face of this onslaught. Red Cloud's killing of Bull Bear had divided the tribe physically as well as emotionally. Those who were now called the "Bear People" had drifted southeast to Nebraska to hunt with the Southern Cheyenne, while the "Smoke People" generally staked camps farther north on the Clear Fork of the Powder River, and often as far east as the White River. When bands from either faction made the trek to Fort John, they were shocked by the out-post's transformation.

In 1849, Chouteau sold the fort to the U.S. government. A company of about fifty officers and enlisted men, called Bluecoats by the natives because of the blue uniforms they wore, were now permanently camped at the once sleepy trad-ing post, which had been renamed again, as Fort Laramie.

Before the Indians' eyes, it had become a western settle-ment where travelers could resupply, find decent medical care, purchase fresh horses, and hire scouts to guide them over the Rockies.

When the soldiers were not drilling or taking target practice, they enlarged the fort's kitchens, warehouses, and corrals; added enlisted men's and officers' quarters; and even constructed a schoolhouse and a wooden bridge spanning the Laramie River. From 1849 to 1851, more than 20,000 wagons trailing over 140,000 head of livestock passed through Fort Laramie, an "Ellis Island of the West" in the center of Lakota land. Now the Indians seethed.

To the Mormons and homesteaders, who had dubbed the Oregon Trail the "Glory Road," the route may have been a godsend—a pathway across the High Plains that led to the promised land. But to the Indians, it was a trail teeming with disease. They believed that these insolent whites were infecting their country not only spiritually, but also—by intention, they were sure—with fatal diseases. The Indians' anger spiked, and emigrants' journals from the era are filled with entries describing all manner of "provocations," from stolen oxen to gruesome killings. The sullen "savages," an emigrant wrote, were now "foes on every hand, subtle as the devil himself."

Sioux braves lurked in butte breaks and amid the papery leaves of thick stands of cottonwoods and oaks, from which they rode down on small parties unlucky enough to have been separated from the main wagon train. At night they sneaked into white camps to drive off horses and cows and steal metal cookware.

They were constantly watching for any pioneer too careless with his weapon. Should he lay his rifle down for even a moment to hitch his oxen team, or to fill his water barrel

First a trading post and then a military post, Wyoming's Fort Laramie was a necessary stopover for wagon trains and other travelers along the Oregon Trail. This illustration was created in 1853.
Courtesy American Heritage Center, University of Wyoming

Settlers in the foothills of the Sierra Nevada Mountains in California. People often walked to lighten the animals' load.
Photo by Lawrence & Houseworth, 1866

from a stream, the rifle would be gone, and perhaps him with it if no one stood lookout. And so ended the days of informal tolls of sugar and coffee in exchange for unbothered passage across the prairie.

Tension was nearing a breaking point. Oddly, the last people to notice this were the soldiers deployed to Fort Laramie, who remained rather oblivious of the Indians' growing anger.

Horse Creek Treaty

A conservative estimate of trailside deaths for 1850 alone is 5,000, meaning that among the optimistic souls departing St. Louis to start a new and better life, one in eleven never made it past the Rockies. Such numbers drew attention back east, and the American government found it necessary to reach out to the tribes, dominated by the Sioux, to come to some agreement regarding right of passage.

The Lakota, however, did not fully understand the enormous number of whites living east of the Mississippi, and considered themselves on an equal footing. This would change, but for now Thomas Fitzpatrick, the former trapper and mountain man familiar with Native customs, acting for the U.S. government, spent the summer crisscrossing the plains from the Arkansas River to the Yellowstone River, spreading word of a grand treaty council to be held near Fort Laramie in September 1851 that would bring peace to the country once and for all.

It was not an easy sell. The western tribes had spent decades raiding and fighting one another. Arikara hated Sioux, Sioux hated Shoshones, Shoshones hated Cheyenne, Cheyenne hated Pawnee. Almost everyone hated the Crows. Now they were being asked to suspend that history, to sit together and pass the peace pipe, to work out boundary agreements set by strange intruders from the East who spoke to them as if they were children.

But Fitzpatrick—a tall, educated Irishman with thick white hair—was respected among the clans. The Indians were impressed with his fighting ability. Called "Broken Hand" by nearly all the tribes, he had earned the nickname in a battle with the Blackfeet during which he had killed seventeen of his pursuers before plunging his horse off a forty-foot cliff into the Yellowstone River and shattering his left wrist.

The Indians would listen to such a fighter, and in time he persuaded nearly every head man to at least hear out the government's plan.

By this point in his life, Red Cloud had served for almost a decade as the Bad Face *blotahunka*. Although the whites from the East probably had no idea that such a revered fighter was in their midst, most if not all of the Indians attending the council knew, respected, and feared him, and many sought him out for the honor of riding and raiding with him. Though he had yet to do battle with whites, it is safe to assume that given his intelligence, leadership, and farsightedness, rather than being intimidated by the 200 Bluecoats parading in their strange squares with modern Hawken rifles and mountain howitzers, Red Cloud was more likely studying the guns that he once called "great medicine."

That September, more than 10,000 men, women, and children from as many as a dozen different tribes gathered about thirty-five miles southeast of Fort Laramie, at the shallow Horse Creek that branched off the North Platte River. The head men rode with dignity, "while braves and boys dashed about, displaying their horsemanship and working off their surplus energy," according to one observer. All the while, the companies of American soldiers positioned themselves between the traveling Sioux and their bitter enemies the Shoshones.

Army engineers had erected a canvas-covered wooden amphitheater along Horse Creek, and toward dusk a column of 1,000 Sioux warriors, four abreast on their war ponies, rode in shouting and singing. The confident Sioux shocked the assemblage by inviting the Shoshones to a great feast of boiled dog. After the meal, the two tribes were joined by the Cheyenne and Arapaho, and all danced and sang until dawn.

The next morning tribal elders, conspicuously unarmed and clad in their finest ceremonial bighorn sheep skins and elk hides, approached a giant flagpole that the soldiers had improvised by lashing together the trunks of three lodgepole pines. The whites looked on as each elder in turn performed a sacred song and danced beneath the fluttering Stars and Stripes. The amphitheater had been left open facing east, and after the head men took their assigned seats, Fitzpatrick had the awkward duty of informing the guests that the supply train hauling presents of tobacco, sugar, coffee, blankets, butcher knives, and bolts of cloth had been delayed leaving St. Louis.

There was some grumbling, but all in all the Indians took it well. No bands departed, and a large red pipe with a three-foot stem was lighted and passed. As each Indian inhaled the mixture of Plains tobacco and bark and berry leaves, he offered elaborate hand signals designed to pay homage to the Great Spirit and to attest that his heart was free from deceit.

Meanwhile, the vast prairie beyond this semicircle was a riot of activity. Indian women made ceremonious trading visits to their tribal enemies' camps, while young braves staged manic horse races, gambled on archery and knife-throwing contests, and flirted with maidens wearing their finest clothes.

On the lush grasslands past the hundreds of lodges that had blossomed like prairie chickweed, preteen boys from each tribe stood sentry over herds of mustangs stretching to the horizon. They eyed one another warily, no doubt recognizing ponies stolen over the years. There were perhaps 2 million wild mustangs loose on the Great Plains at the time, and most tribes were adept at rounding some of them up and training them.

On the morning of September 8, the tribal leaders were invited to the center of the circle, where the formal treaty ceremonies were to take place. After a welcoming ceremony, the Fitzpatrick strode to the center of the semicircle. He introduced the government commissioners, including Col. David Mitchell, the superintendent of Indian Affairs. Framed by the Laramie Mountains scraping the western sky, Mitchell stated his purpose.

Yes, he acknowledged, it was true that the white emigrants passing over Indian lands were thinning the buffalo herds. And, yes, oxen and cattle used to pull their wagons were indeed consuming the grasses. For this, he said, the Great Father in Washington was prepared to make annual payments in the form of hardware, foodstuffs, domestic animals, and agricultural equipment to the Indians, $50,000 worth for each of the next fifty years.

But both sides would have to bend, he emphasized. The tribes must grant future travelers right of passage across the territory as well as allow the U.S. Army to build way stations along the trails west. Finally, he said, the white man was here to help the Indians identify, and learn to respect, territorial boundaries. Civilization was upon them whether they liked it or not, and the constant intertribal slaughter must cease. Colonel Mitchell urged each nation to select one great chief with whom the United States could negotiate these terms.

It is not difficult to imagine the bemusement with which Mitchell's words, once relayed by interpreters, were greeted by warriors like Red Cloud. Why did these confused whites not just tell the wind to stop blowing, the rivers to cease flowing? Red Cloud, the Sioux, and all the western tribes were accustomed to going where they wanted when they wanted, and taking what they wanted on the strength of their courage and cunning.

Red Cloud and the rest were also more than familiar with the promises broken over and over by the white leaders in

"The Great Father in Washington," President Millard Fillmore. *Lithograph by Francis D'Avignon, c. 1850. Daguerreotype by Mathew Brady. Library of Congress*

Red Cloud, about 1880. He is wearing a bone breastplate. *Library of Congress*

Washington. They had only to look south, where the peoples from east of the Mississippi had been forcibly transported to the official Indian Territory in what is now Oklahoma. The Cherokee, Creek, Choctaw, and other forlorn bands lived in a squalid "homeland," scratching out a living on hard dirt, awaiting government handouts like beggars. Worse, the handouts rarely came. This was the future that the Great Father envisioned for the proud Sioux?

Moreover, the idea that any one head man, no matter how well regarded by the tribe, could speak for every brave in every band was incomprehensible to the Sioux. For centuries, their culture had consisted of fluid tribal groups further splintered by the overlapping structures of extended households, camps, and warrior and other societies within bands. Only on buffalo hunts and during formal warfare could leaders impose any kind of discipline on their followers, and even then only rarely. How could the whites not see that one "chief," or two, or even a dozen, could not possibly be a sole ruler?

Meanwhile, more than a week was spent on entertainments and feasts at Horse Creek as the Indians awaited the *wakpamni*, the great distribution of goods. When messengers finally brought news that the gift-laden caravan was a day away, Fitzpatrick and the Indian agent Mitchell reassembled the tribal elders to ask if they had chosen chiefs to represent them. The Indians were sly. They had ridden hundreds of miles and delayed the fall buffalo hunt to receive presents. They were not going to depart empty-handed, even if it meant participating in a sham. They told the whites they had indeed selected representatives. Several men from various tribes stepped forward.

After the conditions of the original treaty were again read aloud and translated—including the unthinkable demand that the Sioux cede to the Crows the territory on either side of the Powder River as it flowed north into the Yellowstone River—an Arapaho head man named Cut Nose more or less spoke for all the tribes when he announced, "I would be glad if the whites would pick out a place for themselves and not come into our grounds. But if they must pass through our country, they should give us game for what they drive off."

On the final day of the council, what was to be known to history as the Horse Creek Treaty was signed to ensure a "lasting peace on the Plains forevermore." After the signing ceremony, the wagon train pulled into camp and formed a circle, and a final grand feast followed the distribution of bribes. Besides the usual gifts of coffee, sugar, and tobacco, sheets of thin brass were distributed; the Sioux liked to cut these into ovals and weave them through their hair.

Finally, the tribes dispersed to the four corners of the territory from which they had arrived.

In his autobiography, Red Cloud does not reveal his thoughts as he, Old Smoke, and the Bad Faces rode north from Horse Creek through the lowering haze of that September morning in 1851. Despite the stipulations in the Horse Creek Treaty, Red Cloud soon enough returned to the lifestyle of all Lakota braves intent on earning glory—hunting buffalo, stealing horses, counting coup, warring on other tribes. It is likely that for a time he gave the grand assembly little more than a passing thought except, perhaps, as a reminder of the plentiful Hawken rifles and deadly cannons the white soldiers possessed.

With his keen eye for weapons, he had also surely noticed that a few of the American officers wore a new type of weapon strapped to their legs, a revolver that fired six times without having to be reloaded. The possibility may have crossed Red Cloud's mind that one day he might have to look down the barrels of those guns.

Red Cloud's Legend Grows

The Lakota had put up an artificial united front at the Horse Creek Treaty Council, largely for the benefit of their white audience. But the Lakota were in fact facing their greatest crisis since stepping out onto the prairie. The buffalo herds were shrinking, the army presence on their lands was multiplying, and the emigrant trains were transmitting diseases that felled entire villages. The Oglalas in particular were so splintered that the northern Smoke People and the Bear People, now hunting as far south as Arkansas, were nearly separate tribes. The growing independence of each served only to weaken the other.

From the white point of view—which was always confused, at best, by the particulars of Indian hierarchy—Red Cloud was too young and obscure to be considered a "chief" as long as men like Old Smoke, Whirlwind, and Old Man Afraid of His Horses still held seats of authority.

The Indians, however, looked at tribal leadership

differently. Red Cloud was undoubtedly the most feared warrior on the High Plains. And though his rank as a *blotahunka* was officially below that of Old Smoke or Whirlwind, in troubled times a warrior's prominence was elevated, in spirit if not in fact. Long before the U.S. government recognized Red Cloud as "chief" of the Lakota, there was a sense among his people that he was their spiritual and military leader.

And if Red Cloud had to literally fight to maintain that position, he would happily do so. There were plenty of opportunities for a man with his wolfish ambition, as the dwindling number of buffalo led to even more competition between the western nations. It also did not hurt that he had acquired a reputation for supernatural powers.

The truth was that Red Cloud worked hard to hone his craft as warrior, hunter, and scout. He taught himself to follow trails by prowling alone, barefoot, over the trackless western prairie through pitch-dark nights, the better to "feel" where an enemy might have trod. And he became so attuned to the natural world that he could "smell" water from even the tiniest shift in wind currents.

Once during a horse raid not long after the killing of Bull Bear, a Pawnee arrow had passed clean through his body. He had recovered swiftly from that wound, and this was much remarked on by friend and foe alike, as were the general good health and good fortune of those who rode with him. And because of his skill at finding game, it was rumored that he could talk to animals, and sometimes even take their form.

Most amazingly, simultaneous Red Cloud "sightings" at impossible distances led to reports that he could either fly or be present in two places at once. Whether or not he cultivated this reputation, it elevated his prestige among a people who set great store by charms, spells, omens, and dreams, and who envisioned only a transparent curtain separating the human and spirit worlds.

Red Cloud did not go out of his way to suppress these rumors of supernatural capabilities, because if such a reputation aided him in his battles against enemies, and in earning even greater honors, such was the way of the Sacred Hoop. On the other hand, not every fight he picked was intended as a strategic maneuver to enhance his tribal standing. Sometimes it just felt good and natural to go out and steal horses. If he took some scalps in the process, so much the better.

10

A Weak Chief

Government Indian agents in the West knew full well that the indigenous peoples' observance of the Horse Creek Treaty had lasted about as long as it took for the ink to dry. But to save their own jobs, they reported few of the constant intertribal raids to the authorities back east. In some cases, the Lakota implored the Indian agents to inform the Great Father that they no longer wished to be held to the pact, that they neither wanted nor needed the American gifts if accepting them meant having to cease their raids on the Arikara and Pawnee or, more insulting, giving up any land to the Crows.

The Hunkpapas, a Sioux tribe being squeezed by farmers pushing up the Missouri River and egged on to retaliate by the charismatic young warrior Sitting Bull, were most unwavering in this regard. They refused to have anything to do with the Indian agent assigned to their tribe, and warned him to stay out of their territory if he valued his scalp.

Sitting Bull, about 1881. He is holding a calumet, a pipe used on ceremonial occasions. *Photo by O. S. (Orlando Scott) Goff, c. 1881, Library of Congress*

The Black Hills, *Paha Sapa,* were named by the Indians because the pine trees that cover them make them look dark from a distance. *The Miriam and Ira D. Wallach Division of Art, Prints and Photographs: Photography Collection, the New York Public Library*

In their reports to Washington, however, the agents never mentioned any of this. Instead, they found more obedient, mostly alcoholic head men loosely associated with the Hunkpapas to sign the receipts for any goods delivered according to the treaty—but not without first taking their own hefty cut of the grain, cattle, and tools.

Unlike Sitting Bull's people, the Lakota continued the ancient warring rituals without much government interference, although Red Cloud and Old Smoke could not completely remove the Bad Faces from the growing white presence clogging the Oregon Trail. The Oglalas continued to be fascinated by these strangers with their funny clothes, odd body odors, and bald heads.

Old Smoke and Red Cloud had for the most part managed to keep their band far north on both sides of the Black Hills during the worst of the cholera, measles, and smallpox outbreaks. But many other Sioux bands were decimated by these diseases, particularly those roaming west of Fort Laramie, where word of the epidemics was slower to arrive. Despite Red Cloud's concocted cure—a combination of boiled red cedar leaves and various other herbs—for these encroaching diseases, it was not nearly enough. One white man on a surveying expedition observed lodge after lodge filled with Lakota corpses.

These outbreaks were one reason the Lakota initially welcomed the arrival of U.S. troops at Fort Laramie. The Indians believed that the soldiers had been dispatched to police and control, if not stop altogether, the wagon trains slithering through their country like long white snakes. They ultimately realized, with astonishment, that the exact opposite was true.

The Bluecoats and their officers cared not a whit for the natives. The soldiers were there to serve the emigrants. If a true leader such as Red Cloud refused to allow his people to visit the army-backed trading posts, the Americans could easily find another, more pliable "chief" to do business with.

Few details from the Indian perspective have emerged about the hazy years immediately before and after the Horse Creek Treaty Council. What is known is that at some point—no one is certain precisely when—the army selected an elderly, obscure Brule head man named Conquering Bear to represent the Lakota as a "chief." The decision was undoubtedly popular with trading post operators. Conquering Bear and his band were regular visitors to the stores and warehouses that had begun to bloom like sage stalks around the soldiers' stockade.

Conquering Bear's elevation further divided the Lakota. As always, the Indians could not conceive of a single man making decisions for all seven Lakota tribes. And even if the idea had any validity—which it did not—if there was going to be a single head man to represent the Lakota, why choose one so far past his fighting prime?

The eastern Lakota—the Miniconjous, Hunkpapas, Sans Arcs, Two Kettles, and Blackfoot Sioux—for the most part ignored Conquering Bear's appointment, or saw it as a good joke on the crazy whites. But the Oglalas, in closer contact with the Americans, were astounded and angry. This was more than just an insult; it was a clear erosion of their autonomy.

Whirlwind, head man of the Oglala Bear People, had inherited many of his father's bullying and obnoxious traits, and he nearly sparked an intertribal war by initially refusing to recognize Conquering Bear as chief. He eventually thought better of alienating the more numerous Brules and relented.

Red Cloud was barely thirty years old and therefore, despite his reputation, could not have expected to be handed so lofty a position. Still, this second snub to his mentor Old Smoke—first by the Oglala council of elders after the killing of Bull Bear, and now by the heedless whites—sat in his stomach like broken glass. By now Old Smoke was in his early seventies, and by all accounts still large, strong, and crafty.

Conquering Bear, however, remained a "chief" in name only, among most Brules. This was further proof to the tribes that adapting to the United States' demands was a fool's game. The newcomers took, and took, and then wanted more. Further hostilities, if not all-out war, with the land-grabbing whites must have seemed inevitable to the Lakota.

For Red Cloud it was merely a question of when and how. It would take a joint strategy to defeat these invaders, as well as a true sense of unity among the squabbling tribes.

This unification was an unlikely proposition. Thus it no doubt occurred to Red Cloud that his best strategy was to stall for time. There was no way, right now, that the Indians could challenge the might of the U.S. Army. He knew well that aside from his own relatively well-armed *akicita,* perhaps one in a hundred Sioux braves owned a gun that worked. As it turned out, when the initial deadly shots were loosed in what would become the decades-long Indian wars on the High Plains, it was the soldiers who killed first.

A Blood-Tinged Season

In June 1853, nearly 2,000 Sioux and Cheyenne arrived at Fort Laramie to stake their lodges amid the ripening blades of grass extending in all directions from the white man's lonely outpost. The Lakota contingent included large delegations of Brules and Oglalas, among them the Bad Faces, as well as a small band of Miniconjous down from the Upper Missouri. All were awaiting delivery of the promised government allotment.

The fort was manned by only thirty or so soldiers, because a detachment of mounted infantry had been deployed to escort one of the year's first Mormon wagon trains rolling into the territory.

It had been a glorious spring, and on the brisk, clear morning of June 15, several Miniconjou braves asked to join a boatload of emigrants who were being ferried across the swift-running North Platte, nearly bursting its banks with snowmelt. The leader of a small squad of Bluecoats assisting the emigrants refused the request, a small scuffle ensued, and a Miniconjou fired a shot.

The musket ball missed its mark, and the offending brave disappeared into a ravine intersecting the prairie. In revenge, that afternoon a platoon of twenty-three soldiers led by an inexperienced second lieutenant named Hugh Fleming rode to the Miniconjous' isolated camp and shot to death at least five braves. It is not known if the troublemaker was among them.

Word spread among the Lakota, and war councils were convened. The Oglala head man Old Man Afraid of His Horses was able to persuade his furious tribesmen—including an influential medicine man, the father of the twelve-year-old Crazy Horse—not to retaliate. Still, members of an arriving Mormon train felt the tension. A homesteader noted in her diary, "We feel this evening that we are in danger. We pray the kind Father to keep us safe this night."

Her prayer was answered, but not those of another settler family camped farther away from the main body of wagons. That night, a party of Sioux crept up to their isolated encampment and killed a husband and wife and their two children. When news of these "most terrible butcheries" reached the fort, another squad of enraged soldiers galloped out of the gates and fired on the first Indians they saw, killing one and wounding another. This led to an age-old Indian conflict—young warriors thirsted for vengeance; older and wiser heads counseled caution.

The Miniconjous in particular were bent on vengeance. Their sentiments were echoed by Sitting Bull and the

Hunkpapas. The headstrong Sitting Bull, now thirty-two, had counted his first coup at the age of fourteen, when he had disobeyed his father and joined a raiding party against the Crows. He had since grown into a skilled fighter as well as a holy *wicasa wakan,* or "vision seeker," and had performed the Sun Dance numerous times. His voice carried weight, but not enough to convince the Oglalas and Brules—who were much more familiar with the army's firepower and who urged accommodation.

In the end, back at Fort Laramie, the "chief" Conquering Bear proposed a radical solution. The Lakota, he said, should petition the Great Father in Washington to reconsider his policy of stationing such small, ill-trained, poorly led, and easily spooked troops in the middle of a territory granted to the Lakota by the white man's own treaty.

Red Cloud was not happy with this compromise, which he perceived as a groveling response. His influence over the Lakota would carry much greater force in a decade, but for now he remained silent and went along with the plan, with a mixture of disappointment and anger. Given the apparent spinelessness of so many of the Sioux head men, as well as their inability to reach agreements, he recognized that this was not the best moment to speak up. As it happened, the blood-tinged events of the following summer proved beyond his control.

In August 1854, the Lakota returned to the grasslands on the North Platte, again in anticipation of the army freight wagons hauling the seasonal endowments. This time they staked camp a cautious distance south of Fort Laramie. The post's duty roster had increased to forty troopers and two officers—the twenty-eight-year-old commander Fleming, now a first lieutenant, and his aggressive subordinate Lt. John Grattan. The same small band of Miniconjous were again present; they camped close to a large contingent of Brules.

One afternoon, a Mormon wagon train was passing nearby when a worn-out, footsore cow wandered in among the Miniconjou lodges. A pack of dogs cornered the lame animal. Its terrified owner dared not retrieve it. A Miniconjou man shot the cow, butchered it, and shared the stringy meat with his band.

In the white man's eyes, Conquering Bear was still the "chief" of all the Lakota, and when word of this seemingly inconsequential event reached him, he sensed trouble. He acted immediately to head it off by riding into Fort Laramie and offering payment for the cow. Lieutenant Fleming instead insisted that the offending Miniconjou turn himself in. Conquering Bear was incredulous. Not only was the scrawny animal not worth a fight, Conquering Bear was also acting in accordance with the Horse Creek Treaty. A provision stated that in the case of an Indian offense against a white civilian, the offending tribe, through its chief, should offer a solution.

In a last-ditch effort at reconciliation, Conquering Bear told Fleming that he would try to persuade the offending Miniconjou to turn himself in. This was an extraordinary offer, and Conquering Bear must have known it was useless. No Indian, and especially no Sioux, would willingly allow himself to be taken to the Bluecoat jail. An Indian would rather die fighting.

Conquering Bear's incredible offer indicates that he was aware of what could happen if the soldiers provoked another confrontation. But young Lt. Fleming was agitated. The next morning, egged on by Lt. Grattan, Fleming ordered his subordinate to lead a troop to the Brule-Miniconjou village and seize the cow-killer. In Grattan's view, the white race would always trump the Indians, no matter the numerical odds.

Grattan readied a twelve-pound field gun and a snub-nosed mountain howitzer, and called for volunteers. All forty infantrymen stepped forward. He selected twenty-nine to mount up. He also summoned a mixed-race interpreter named Wyuse, whose mother was a member of the smaller tribe that hated the Sioux. Wyuse was so drunk he had to be lifted onto his saddle. Along the trail, this motley procession halted at a small trading post operated by a stout man named James Bordeaux. Lt. Grattan tried to convince the veteran trapper to join him.

Bordeaux, who had married a Brule, was wise in the ways of the Indians. He eyed the clusters of mounted Sioux flanking the troop on the red-earth bluffs overlooking the rutted road—including, by his own admission, Red Cloud's Bad Faces—and declined to join the soldiers. Bordeaux did offer Grattan one piece of advice: gag your drunken interpreter.

Between the gates of Fort Laramie and Grattan's destination stood at least 300 Oglala lodges, another 200 Brule lodges, and finally the 20 Miniconjou lodges next to a smaller

An illustration from an 1851 encyclopedia shows artillery wagons, caissons carrying chests of ammunition, and traveling forges.
Library of Congress

contingent of 80 Brule tepees. Five thousand Indians. Twelve hundred warriors. Still, on nearing the Miniconjou camp, Wyuse galloped ahead roaring insults and threatening to eat the heart of every Lakota before sundown.

Conquering Bear attempted one final negotiation. He met Lt. Grattan at the edge of the Miniconjou camp as the officer positioned his artillery, and asked him to hold his fire while he made a last appeal to the offending man who had killed the cow. Later, there were reports that Wyuse intentionally mistranslated these last words.

As the old "chief" rode away, Lt. Grattan lost what little patience he had started with, particularly after seeing half a dozen Indians begin priming their muskets. He ordered his men to form a skirmish line. One went a step further, and aimed his rifle and fired. A brave tipped over dead. At this Grattan ordered a volley loosed into the village. The rifle reports surprised Conquering Bear, who turned and tried to wave Grattan off. The old man was standing tall in the center of the camp, urging his tribesmen not to return fire, when the howitzers boomed and another rifle volley echoed. Grapeshot splintered several lodgepoles, and Conquering Bear fell, mortally wounded.

It was over in minutes. Rifle balls and clouds of arrows as thick as black flies sailed into the American line. Lt. Grattan and most of his men were killed on the spot. A few wounded Bluecoats managed to swing up onto horses or crawl into the artillery wagon to try to flee back up the trail. One, punctured by seven arrow and musket holes, made it as far as Bordeaux's trading post, where he staggered inside and hid in a closet. He later died from his wounds. The rest were swarmed by Brules and Miniconjous galloping up the road as well as by a separate wave of Oglalas led by Red Cloud and his *akicita* sweeping down from the bluffs. The army soldiers were dead by the time the whirling dust clouds kicked up by the horses had settled. Odds are, Red Cloud killed his first white man that day.

Hostilities only escalated from that point on. In November, a small party of Brules from Conquering Bear's clan attacked a mail coach on the Oregon Trail south of Fort Laramie. The raiders were led by a half-Brule warrior named Spotted Tail, a famous fighter who, though two years younger than Red Cloud, also led his band's *akicita* and was said to have already taken more than a hundred scalps. Spotted Tail ordered the two coach drivers and a luckless passenger killed and mutilated, and a strongbox containing $20,000 in gold coins was taken.

Later that winter, Spotted Tail sent out representatives carrying the war pipe. Some Miniconjous and Hunkpapas, including Sitting Bull's clan, were receptive. But on the whole the riders returned frustrated. Most of Conquering Bear's Brule kinsmen and nearly all of the Oglalas, including Red Cloud and the Bad Faces, considered the fight with Lt. Grattan an isolated affair for which revenge had been taken.

Not so the whites. Calls to avenge the "murders" of young Grattan and his men spread like ripples on a lake all the way to Washington, D.C., where the causes and effects of their deaths were debated in Congress. Moreover, the St. Louis shipping companies, spooked by the mail coach raid and the missing strongbox money, used the deaths to convince politicians to send more federal troops to clean out the "savage" threat. Indian agents, silent at first but now sensing their usefulness ending, protested. It was too late. The American government's hand had been forced.

12

The Proudest Moment

In the early summer of 1855, Red Cloud, now thirty-four years old, was granted the highest social and political honor extended to a Sioux warrior. After long years of striving, he was finally asked to become a part of what passed for the Lakota aristocracy, in an elaborate public Pipe Dance ritual called the *hunka*. The ceremony was attended by all the Oglala bands except one, Whirlwind's Kiyuska. Though Old Smoke was still alive and hearty, the invitation was the clearest signal that the tribe considered Red Cloud a future head man.

The Bad Faces moved north toward the White River in South Dakota where the *hunka* ceremony was to be held. They joined the entire Oglala tribe on rolling grassland along the banks of the river in preparation for the Pipe Dance. The ritual that followed, while not officially anointing Red Cloud as Old Smoke's successor, certainly made him eligible.

Given his modest heritage, even a few decades earlier

this would have seemed impossible. But these were desperate times for the Lakota, and Red Cloud's fighting skills and wealth of horses allowed for such an exception. It was a good political start for the *blotahunka.*

After several days of feasting, tribal elders planted a three-foot-wide tree stump gilded with gypsum, a sacred mineral, in the center of the vast area. The Oglalas—men, women, and children—encircled this holy table, leaving openings on opposite ends. Through the eastern portal marched the tribe's head men and shamans adorned in their most lavish finery, feathers, and paint. Simultaneously, a procession of men, including Red Cloud, entered from the west, naked except for small breechcloths.

At a signal from a sacred drum the head men, according to seniority, peeled off from the shamans and formed a line that wound past the altar and in front of the candidates. Each head man placed his palm on each applicant's forehead as a symbol of his worthiness and submission to the Great Spirit. Then, still in single file, the older men returned to the east side of the altar, took up a gourd of water, and again approached the applicants, one standing before each to wash first his face, then his hands, then his feet.

When the head men returned to their original positions the shamans stepped forward, one by one, performing ancient, elaborate dance steps and flourishing a single eagle feather in the direction of the four compass points. Each laid his right palm flat on the symbolic stump, and with his left hand pointed to the sun while vowing to the Great Spirit that his heart was pure. He emphasized that he had never lied to injure his people, nor ever spilled the blood of any tribesman. He intoned that he expected the same from the men who were about to join the leadership class.

This shaman then moved to the other side of the altar, removed a small bag of paint from his belt, and dabbed the face of the first candidate. While that was occurring, another shaman moved to the stump in the same manner and made the same vows; and by the time the first had moved on to paint the next face, the second was painting the first candidate's hands and arms.

And so it went with a third shaman, who spread paint over the legs of the applicants from knees to feet. A fourth shaman followed, anointing each candidate's face and head with holy oil. Finally, the tribe's most celebrated priest stepped forward. After making the vows at the altar, he swept his hands over the heads of the followers. In a voice that all the tribe could hear, he issued a sermon driving home the great duties and responsibilities the electees owed to the Sioux peoples by virtue of their new, exalted position.

The head men then took their new brethren by the hands and led them into a semicircle on the east side of the altar. The high priest removed from his pouch a handful of downy eagle feathers, which had been plucked from the underside of the bird's wing, and attached one to each man's head. The ceremony was complete; the men had been elevated to the chieftain class. As the tribe's best dancers burst from the crowd to wind around the holy tree stump, another round of feasting began.

When Red Cloud later recounted this ceremony, he

described it as one of the proudest moments of his life. Yet his joy, he wrote, was not for himself. Not only had the ritual promoted individual warriors to an elevated class; it also affected their male children. This meant that his only son, Jack Red Cloud—the fourth of his five children with Pretty Owl—would not have to experience the prejudice that had stood in his own path to leadership. Of course, if the whites had their way in that summer of 1855, his hopes and dreams for his son would be of no consequence.

Breaking Point

While the Oglalas were gathered for the
Pipe Dance, their cousins were busy. The Brules in particular,
led by the charismatic Spotted Tail, stepped up their raids to
steal livestock from the settlers' trains—helped later in the
summer by Oglala bands returning from the *hunka*. Spotted
Tail had taken his name as a boy when a trapper presented
him with the gift of a raccoon tail, and he wore it on every
raid. It became a familiar sight to whites traveling the Glory
Road.

In June 1855, a group of Miniconjous intercepted a wagon
train passing through a tight ravine on the trail. When the
wagon master rode out to greet them with the usual gifts of
sugar and coffee, they shot him through the heart. A few days
later the same Indians, eighteen braves in all, swooped down
on another train and ran off with sixteen horses. During
the chaos, an oxcart driven by a husband and wife became
separated from the main body; the Indians surrounded

it and relentlessly thrust their spears into the couple.

A group of horrified Oglala head men later returned the stolen stock, and even organized a general Lakota offensive against the Omahas in hopes of distracting their braves from further violence against white settlers. But the damage had been done. That August, a year to the day of the Grattan massacre, a new Indian agent, named Thomas Twiss, rode into Fort Laramie.

Twiss's first official proclamation was to declare the nearby North Platte River a literal "deadline." He dispatched riders to inform the Lakota and their allies that any Indians found north of the winding river would be considered hostile and killed on the spot. Though much of the prime buffalo range was in this area, many Brules and almost all the Oglalas rode south and made camp near the post. The tribes and bands of Oglalas and Brules who did "come in" initially staked separate camps on either side of Fort Laramie, but Twiss forced them to combine their 400 lodges into one huge village thirty-five miles north of the stockade.

Red Cloud never mentions in his autobiography whether he obeyed Twiss's order, and there were no witnesses to his presence at Fort Laramie that summer. In his recollections, however, he hints that in a pinch he would be off hunting or raiding in the no-man's-land west of the fort.

Soon, Twiss rode out to address the head men. He told them that he knew the names of the Brules who had attacked and stolen the gold coins from the mail coach, and promised that they would face swift and certain justice, as would any Indian who left this safe harbor and recrossed the North

Platte. As Twiss spoke, a column of 600 infantry and cavalry troops had already begun a stealthy march out of Fort Leavenworth in eastern Kansas, bound for Sioux territory.

The Indians suffered another indignity in March 1856, when the Lakota head men were summoned from their winter camps to a council at Fort Laramie. There they were instructed by Twiss to return any property and livestock stolen from whites and to end all harassment of emigrants along the Oregon Trail—a virtual surrender of the once buffalo-rich Platte River valley. Any Indian found harassing travelers along this road would be taken to prison in chains. And so the remains of the Horse Creek Treaty were buried, just five years after it had been signed.

For nearly four decades the Lakota had put up with traders, trappers, soldiers, and emigrants trespassing on their lands. They had been literally sickened to death by white interlopers, and when they protested, they had been given promises that the whites never intended to keep. They had watched the buffalo herds recede as homesteaders advanced along the Missouri. They had seen the whites turn on a head man they themselves had appointed and kill him over an old cow. They had witnessed friendly tribes attacked by soldiers, and their women and children captured, assaulted, and murdered.

The Lakota finally recognized that something big, something momentous never before considered, must be done. So it happened that riders were sent out to summon all the Lakota tribes to a grand council to be held the following summer after the spring buffalo hunt.

Lakota Council

In August 1857, more Lakota congregated along the placid Belle Fourche River than had attended the Horse Creek Treaty Council six years earlier. For 10,000 years, bands of indigenous North Americans had made pilgrimages to this holy ground in present-day western South Dakota where the stark Bear Butte loomed high over the riverbanks.

To the Cheyenne this rock was the sacred Giving Hill, the height from which the Great Spirit had imparted the "sweet medicine" of life to the tribe. This belief influenced later Sioux arrivals, who considered the remains of this ancient volcanic eruption a holy place of meditation despite placing their own origin myth farther south, in the Black Hills. But never before had the Lakota come together at Bear Butte, or anywhere on the Plains, as a single people.

This gathering included the Oglalas, Miniconjous, and Brules, but also the northern tribes—the Sans Arcs, Black-foot Sioux, Two Kettles, and Hunkpapas—who set a tone of defiance. By some estimates, as many as 10,000 Indians were present, more than three quarters of the total population of Lakota. They had gathered under a domed blue sky to fashion a "national" policy for dealing with the American aggressors. The lodges were arranged in a huge oval around the southern rim of the barren stone tower at Bear Butte, and as young men raced horses, gambled, and purified themselves in preparation for a multi-tribal dance, they took time to gawk at heroes they knew only from legend. Here was the fierce Hump, the mighty Blackfoot whose future was said to have been foretold when as a boy he strayed into a cave and stared down a great gray wolf. Hump was conferring with his handsome tribesman Long Mandan, whose clear, wide-set eyes sparkled above sharp cheekbones. Young and old alike tilted their heads to stare up at the seven-foot Miniconjou fighter Touch the Clouds, who walked in the manner of a praying mantis, lifting his legs so high that he appeared to be using them as feelers. Packs of snapping dogs followed the fierce Hunkpapa "Shirt Wearer" Four Horns, who wore a necklace of raw meat across his hair-fringed tunic and was accompanied nearly everywhere he went by his nephew Sitting Bull. In each lodge they visited, these two preached war against the whites.

Red Cloud and other revered members of the western Oglala bands, such as the father and son Old Man Afraid of His Horses and Young Man Afraid of His Horses, introduced themselves to eastern counterparts like the seasoned fighter Crow Feather of the Sans Arcs. Over many council fires and private feasts, the Indians debated about what to do with the Americans.

Old Man Afraid of His Horses, a senior Oglala head man, hoped his son would succeed him but instead saw the warrior chief Red Cloud rise to the leadership role. *Courtesy American Heritage Center, University of Wyoming*

Young Man Afraid of His Horses, son of Old Man Afraid of His Horses and a grandson of Old Smoke, fought alongside Red Cloud in the 1866–68 war. *Courtesy National Anthropological Archives, Smithsonian Institution*

Militants like Red Cloud and Sitting Bull lobbied separately and together for immediate raids against army units and settler wagon trains. Moderates such as Old Man Afraid of His Horses and a Hunkpapa head man named Bear's Rib urged restraint, arguing that the whites seemed content to have secured their "holy road." The moderates would fight if they must, they said, but why disturb a hornet's nest? Red Cloud and his allies countered that it was only a matter of time before these white wasps again flew as a swarm in search of larger Indian orchards. When had the Indian, Red Cloud asked, ever known the whites to be satisfied with the lands that they already possessed?

Despite these disagreements, one unifying strategic goal did emerge: continued protection, by force if necessary, of the sanctity of the most sacred Black Hills. Oaths were sworn to defend the cherished *Paha Sapa* from all white intrusions, and the festivities remained generally upbeat and positive.

When Crazy Horse related tales that he had heard from the Cheyenne of Bluecoat guns that fired six times without having to be reloaded, Red Cloud remembered seeing those very same weapons at the gathering at Horse Creek six years earlier. Whatever apprehension Red Cloud felt, however, may have been overridden by the decisions made by the Lakota head men at Bear Butte. By the time the thousands of Indian ponies had reduced the prairie grass to nubs in all directions, it was decided that each tribe would stake out its own new hunting ground to develop and defend. The Oglalas chose Powder River.

New Land

The days of the Oglalas' annual spring buffalo hunt from the Black Hills east to the Missouri River had long ended. White settlers had converted the fertile floodplain in the state of Iowa and in the Kansas, Nebraska, and Dakota Territories into one long string of farms and small communities.

By 1857, when the Sioux met at Bear Butte, nearly two dozen steamboats were in regular service between St. Louis, Missouri, and Sioux City, Iowa. With the homesteaders encroaching on the Lakota from the east while army troops stepped up patrols along the Oregon Trail to the south, the Lakota had no choice but to retreat north and west, deeper into the rich buffalo grounds bordering the Yellowstone and Bighorn ranges on lands held by the Crows, the Shoshones, the Nez Percé, and the northern Arapaho.

The Powder River Country had the most unspoiled hunting grounds in North America, and the Oglala took advantage of these bounties. Their society grew wealthier and stronger, and so too did Red Cloud's grip on power. Warriors from other Oglala bands now vied to ride with him against the Crows and other enemies, and each fighting season he attracted greater numbers of Brules, Miniconjous, and even Sans Arcs and Hunkpapas to join his far-reaching expeditions. These companions included Crazy Horse.

Red Cloud's military leadership also took on a new form and function. He could not afford to lead a few braves on raids merely for glory and plunder. His war parties for the first time also hunted for Indian "intruders" to expel from the Lakota's burgeoning empire. This often meant deviating from the traditional Lakota method of prairie warfare on open, flat terrain.

On one occasion, for instance, his scouts picked up fresh Shoshone moccasin tracks along the base of the Bighorns in northern Wyoming. Red Cloud and about seventy-five braves caught up to the Shoshones and chased them back into the mountains.

In the old days, that would have been warning enough. Not now. Red Cloud ordered his Sioux to dismount and tie their horses, and they pursued the Shoshones on foot up the steep mountainside. A running high country battle through thick pine and blue spruce ensued. When the Shoshones disappeared behind a circular wall of boulders that formed a natural fortress on top of a rocky promenade, Red Cloud's braves surrounded them.

For a day and night the Lakota besieged the Shoshones, feinting, charging, being beaten back, each side's sharpshooters firing whenever an enemy exposed himself. Occasionally a Sioux arrow would lodge in a Shoshone's head as it was raised over the top of the wall. For the most part, however, the Shoshones holding the high ground got the better of the fight as the Bad Faces, still mired in the ways of prairie warfare, failed to press their psychological advantage.

So excited were the Oglala braves guarding the rear of the makeshift fort that they abandoned their positions to charge, leaving open a back door—through which most of the Shoshones escaped into the forest. Red Cloud was furious. But all he could do was file away the episode and ensure that it never happened again. The Oglala war party climbed down the mountain, retrieved their horses, and rode back and forth along the foot of the range for three days as a signal to any Indians who might be watching that this was now Lakota land. This, too, was something new.

16

Head Man

By the end of the 1850s, Red Cloud was head man of the Bad Face Oglalas in all but name. At age eighty-two, Old Smoke was no longer an active leader. Though novice army officers deployed to Fort Laramie continued to recognize the more pliant Old Man Afraid of His Horses as "chief" of the Sioux—Red Cloud's name had yet to appear in any official government reports—most Lakota, including many from the far Missouri River regions east of the Black Hills, considered Red Cloud their military and spiritual leader.

This designation carried a heavy responsibility. The history of the white invasion had demonstrated that individual bands could not stand alone against the might of the American army. But could a multi-tribal alliance actually be formed to battle the intruders? And if so, what were its chances of prevailing?

Of one fact Red Cloud was certain: large-scale engage– ments against the Bluecoats where the two sides were of equal numbers were essentially suicide missions. The only way to fight them was to gather enough of the squabbling Sioux under one banner and use overwhelming force against any smaller targets that presented themselves. They would apply their knowledge of the country to run off army horse and cattle herds, and starve the Bluecoats out of their isolated forts.

It would be a war of decoy and ambush, of fighting from bluff to butte and from coulee to creek bed—in short, a guerrilla war before such a term was actually used. It was, Red Cloud recognized, the Indians' only recourse.

Still, how could he convince the different tribes of Indians, particularly his own people? Despite the occasional trespasses by greedy white hunters, the Lakota were experiencing a calm period. With their enemies, particularly the Crows, cleared from the mile-high Powder River Country, the Lakota were free to roam an immense short-grass prairie bursting with buffalo, antelope, elk, deer, and bighorn sheep and crossed by abundant sources of sweet water, flowing out of pine-covered mountains. During the broiling summer months, cool mountain meadows awash with goldenrod and black-eyed Susans beckoned, and in winter, the south face of the Black Hills served as a gigantic windbreak against the numbing gales from the Canadian flats.

Just as Old Man Afraid of His Horses had argued at Bear Butte, the Bluecoats had not strayed far from their line of forts and mail stations along the Oregon Trail. Even the rough dirt road that the new army commander of the Northwest Territories—the Indian-hating general William Selby

American artist George Catlin's 1850 sketch of wild horses.
Rare Book Division, the New York Public Library

Fresh water tumbles from the Black Hills.
George Arents Collection, the New York Public Library

Harney—had blazed from Fort Laramie to South Dakota's Fort Pierre in 1855 was now growing over; the ruts from the army freight wagons were barely visible beneath carpets of white prairie clover and purple asters.

Given the circumstances, it would be hard to make the case for war on the whites. As it was, Red Cloud and the Lakota had no way of knowing that far to the east, two American armies were already preparing for an epic Civil War that would, only temporarily, push the "Indian problem" far down on the government's list of priorities.

The Dakotas Rise

The distant echoes of the bombardment of Fort Sumter on April 12, 1861, reverberated well beyond the Mississippi. At the start of the American Civil War, officers from Southern states who were stationed on the Plains resigned en masse; 313 of them headed home to fight for the Confederacy. Most of the noncommissioned officers and enlisted men remained true to the Union, but they, too, rapidly disappeared from the territories.

Even the detachment at Fort Laramie, now the western communications hub connecting the coasts, was reduced to a skeleton company of about 130 soldiers as battalions and regiments from across the West marched home. The few Southern officers who did not give up their commissions were viewed with suspicion by the War Department.

The Lakota made no deliberate effort to exploit the War Between the States. Rumors, however, spread to Washington of Confederate agents fueling insurrection among the tribes,

This drawing from the January 24, 1863, edition of *Frank Leslie's Illustrated Newspaper* depicts the mass hanging of thirty-eight Dakota Sioux in Mankato, Minnesota. *Courtesy American Antiquarian Society*

particularly the Sioux, the Cheyenne, and, farther south, the peoples occupying the Indian Territory of present-day Oklahoma. In keeping with the government's usual incomprehension of Indian beliefs, none of the fearmongers gave a thought to why Indians would ever fight for a slaveholding republic. In any case, the South lacked the money and manpower to organize an Indian uprising.

The exception was in Minnesota. In the summer of 1862, conflict erupted and was put down with brutal efficiency, but not before much blood—most of it innocent Indian—was spilled. The number of white civilians and soldiers killed in the Dakota War ranged as high as 800. Indian dead were undoubtedly much more numerous; no one bothered to count them.

The war's impact on the eastern Sioux, however, went deeper than its death toll. The once mighty Dakotas were now a society in pieces. And because those survivors who did manage to reach the prairie lands of their western cousins related their stories, a feeling of foreboding hung over the Lakota camps of the Upper Missouri and the Powder River Country.

PART THREE

The
Resistance

Force, no matter how concealed, begets resistance.

—*Lakota proverb*

Taming Land

Two years into the American Civil War, the tension between whites and Indians increased dramatically. In the early 1860s, gold was discovered in great quantities in the craggy mountain canyons of western Montana. Thousands of hopefuls had already made their way to shanty boomtowns of that territory's "Fourteen-Mile City" by traveling a twisting route to avoid Sioux territory. But the most direct path to the goldfields ran directly through Red Cloud's land, which had been deeded to his people by treaty. In 1862, President Lincoln rallied Congress to pass the Homestead Act. It allowed that any U.S. citizen, including freed slaves and female heads of households, could take title to 160 acres of government land west of the Mississippi River, provided he or she lived on it for five years in a row. It cost $18 to file a land claim.

The trails west, already swollen with fortune hunters and men hoping to avoid military service, as well as with the more than 300,000 deserters from the Union and Confederate armies, were now joined by families lugging seed drills and steel plows that would slice open the prairie. The population of the West soon doubled.

The settlers, most loyal to Lincoln and the Union, wanted roads and telegraph lines, stage coach and mail service, and above all protection against the Indians. Lincoln was a shrewd politician with an eye toward a second term. There was no question about his response, as Northern volunteers who had enlisted to fight the Confederates instead found themselves marching on what the eastern newspapers called "red pagans."

President Lincoln needed gold and silver from the mountain territories to pay for the war. It was essential that he provide military escorts both for the miners heading west to Montana, Colorado, Nevada, and Idaho and for the caravans bringing the ore back to the East. The army also needed to protect the gold mines that were close to Southern states from being captured by the Confederates. The government built a series of new posts and fortified camps running from Omaha to Salt Lake City. These posts, established on Indian land, served to further inflame the western tribes. The army presence west of the Missouri River steadily increased.

Through this period, Red Cloud's Powder River Country was perhaps the only peaceful area in the West. The great Oglala warrior chief recognized that this peace was temporary. For many years, he had anticipated a war and its consequences, mentally sifting the possible outcomes like the gold miners panning mountain streams.

Abraham Lincoln, President of the United States, 1861–1865.
Photo by Anthony Berger, February 9, 1864, Library of Congress

Fort Laramie, Wyoming, as it looked in 1868. It had grown
from a military fort to become a small town with a school and
medical building. *Photo by Alexander Gardner, the Miriam and
Ira D. Wallach Division of Art, Prints and Photographs: Photography
Collection, the New York Public Library*

While the Union and Confederate armies savaged each other in the East, Indian groups grew increasingly turbulent and vicious on both sides of the Oglalas' tranquil Powder River territory. In Colorado, the Ute had taken to raiding and burning stage stations leading into Denver, and in the northern Rockies, the Shoshones and Bannocks declared open hostilities on gold seekers drilling more and deeper holes into their mountains.

Across the Kansas-Nebraska frontier, Cheyenne Dog Soldiers were killing homesteaders and frequently kidnapping women and children. The Comanche and Kiowa virtually closed the Santa Fe Trail, and there were rumors that representatives from those great southern tribes were traveling to the Oklahoma Territory to stir up an Indian insurrection there.

On the Upper Missouri, Sitting Bull and his ferocious Hunkpapas attacked traders, ranchers, and farmers brave enough to settle on the country's most windswept prairie. Twice that summer, combined Hunkpapa-Dakota war parties ambushed cavalry detachments that were escorting wagon trains of miners to the gold camps of Virginia City in western Montana. During the second attack, they forced a company of Iowa soldiers nearly all the way back to Sioux City.

As news of Sitting Bull's activities spread to the Powder River Country, small bands of Miniconjous, Sans Arcs, and Blackfoot Sioux, and even some Oglalas, began making raids of their own. The few miners foolhardy enough to make for Montana via Nebraska and Wyoming were scalped and dismembered, mail coaches were destroyed, and army supply wagons were looted and burned.

Finally, in August 1864, General Alfred Sully, a Philadelphia watercolorist and oil painter, led a column of 2,500 men into North Dakota and defeated Sitting Bull's Sioux in a savage three-day battle. In the end, the Hunkpapas and Dakotas had no answer for the firepower of Sully's artillery. Sully personally ordered the bodies of three braves thought to have been Sitting Bull's closest advisors decapitated. Their severed heads were fixed on poles and left behind as a warning. This was a turning point. The defeat forced the North Dakota peoples to migrate southwest toward the Black Hills, bringing them closer to Red Cloud.

First Steps

During this time, Red Cloud and his people showed no inclination to disrupt the status quo. Relatively undisturbed in their new territory on the Upper Powder, free of the white man's whiskey and diseases, the Oglalas and their Brule cousins reveled in the return to a more pure and natural lifestyle, the open spaces of the high prairie corresponding to some mystical place within the Sacred Hoop. They passed the seasons hunting in the majestic, game-laden territory and making occasional raids on the Crows and Shoshones—by now pushed almost beyond the Bighorns—before settling into cozy winter camps, where the larders were piled high with venison and buffalo meat.

Even when a regiment of infantry and five companies of cavalry were deployed from California to Fort Laramie to protect the overland mail route along the Oregon Trail, the Bad Faces maintained a tentative peace with the soldiers.

. . .

After General Sully's victory over Sitting Bull, Lincoln sent additional volunteers from across the Midwest to man key crossings along the Missouri, Platte, and Arkansas Rivers. The Minnesota Uprising may have been the root of the Indian wars that would engulf the High Plains for most of the next decade, but those wars were also encouraged by a series of ill-considered appointments of general officers on the other side of the Mississippi.

For all their wrongheaded racial attitudes, the earlier generation of engineer-soldiers had attempted to administer a bit of justice to the West's Native peoples. The officers now deployed to the frontier included not only those the War Department could spare from more important fighting against the South, but also men who believed the American army far superior to any indigenous force. These men ranged from naive to stupid to hateful.

One frontier general admitted that he knew nothing about Indians and did not care to learn anything. It was not unusual for his troops to conduct target practice on passing, peaceful Indian bands, or for his jumpy junior officers to order attacks on their own uniformed Pawnee scouts. These generals and their staffs showed no ability to control their troops.

Lieutenant Caspar Collins and his company of Ohio cavalry were among the new arrivals at Fort Laramie. As a child, Collins had dreamed of fighting Indians, and when he came west in 1862, he was impatient for the opportunity. His men were so influenced by the Indian-fighting tales that many began to imagine themselves frontiersmen.

The arrival of the famed mountain man Jim Bridger at

Fort Laramie increased the recruits' desire for action. Bridger became the Frontier Army's chief scout at $10 a day, more than most officers were paid.

Some who knew him thought that the sixty-year-old Bridger was finally showing his age. When he was young, his standard meal might include an entire side of buffalo ribs. Now he was content with a jackrabbit and an eighteen-inch trout roasted on spits over a campfire and a quart of coffee to wash them down.

Nonetheless, the new officers and enlisted men alike were in awe of Bridger's eccentric skills. He could find fresh water on the driest flats, build and feed a fire in a winter whiteout, and safely guide a wagon team across a quicksand-laden river. He also showed the newcomers an old Indian trick: ridding their clothing of ever-present fleas and lice by spreading the garments over anthills.

On one occasion, Bridger led a troop to the site of an attack on a settler's wagon near the South Pass through the Rockies. A father and son had been killed and butchered, their bodies left splayed across the buffalo grass near a copse of box elders. The attackers had not taken the younger man's navy Colt.

Bridger dismounted and examined the mutilated corpses, which were pierced by arrows that he identified as Cheyenne and Arapaho. He pried the revolver, its chamber empty, from the son's hand and walked slowly in ever-expanding circles. Soon, with a flourish, he snapped off a branch of sagebrush. There was a speck of blood on it. Bridger beamed. "The boy hit one of the scamps, anyway," he said.

A long line of wagons bringing Mormon settlers to the Utah Territory in 1847. *Library of Congress*

Jim Bridger was the ultimate example of the early 1800s mountain man who blazed trails, scouted for the U.S. Army, and sometimes helped in negotiations. *Courtesy American Heritage Center, University of Wyoming*

It did not take long for "Major" Bridger to achieve cult status. One of Lt. Caspar Collins's letters to his mother describes Bridger and his acolytes in their "big white hats with beaver around it; a loose white coat of buck or antelope skins, trimmed fantastically with beaver fur; buffalo breeches, with strings hanging from ornaments along the sides; a Mexican saddle, moccasins, and spurs. . . . They have bridles with ten dollars' worth of silver ornaments on; Indian ponies, a heavy rifle, a Navy revolver, a hatchet and a Bowie knife."

It is no wonder that many of the young enlisted men in Collins's company soon discarded their blue woolens in favor of buckskins and Spanish spurs, and purchased hardy Indian ponies out of their own base pay of $14 a month.

But the arrival of American troops would not be the first troubling omens for the Lakota way of life. In 1863, a single wagon train veered north off the Oregon Trail and rolled up the center of the Powder River Country. Lakota and Cheyenne scouts posted on the pine-studded foothills of the Bighorns halted the line of prairie schooners and signed a demand to speak to its leader. A tall, lanky twenty-eight-year-old and his Mexican interpreter rode out to meet them.

The interpreter introduced the wagon master as "Captain" John Bozeman. Bozeman tipped his hat, revealing a thick blond mane, and told the Indians that he did not intend to settle their land but merely meant to pass through it en route to the new mining digs beyond the mountains in western Montana. The Lakota emphatically refused. "You are going into our country where we hunt," an old chief said. "Your people have taken the rest. Along the great road to the south,

John Bozeman (above) and John Jacobs followed
old buffalo paths to establish the Bozeman Trail,
which in its short life provided a passage to
Montana for thousands of gold seekers and settlers.
*Courtesy American Heritage Center, University of
Wyoming*

white men have driven away all the buffalo and antelope. We won't let you do that here. . . . If you go into our hunting country, our people will wipe you out."

Bozeman returned to the train and urged the group to call the Indians' bluff, but the travelers were wary. They argued for ten days over whether to proceed. In the end, they voted to turn back and instead follow the uncontested, if longer and more difficult, route to Montana that snaked west of the mountains.

As the Indians watched the train disappear over the southern horizon, they could not have known that Bozeman, a failed gold miner from Georgia, had just taken the first step in his plan. Four months earlier, he and a frontiersman named John Jacobs had traced ancient buffalo and Indian paths to find a faster way to Montana. The route they proposed, which shaved 400 miles off the previous route, angled north by northwest from the long-established Oregon Trail directly through the heart of sacred Indian hunting grounds teeming with game. But above all, it was one of the last sanctuaries of the great northern herd of sacred buffalo, millions upon millions of which migrated through the territory.

Bozeman was a persistent man, and not easily discouraged by the threat of losing his handsome blond hair. The indifference of the Lakota in dealing with him that July day would return to haunt them. From the faint wheel ruts dug by that first wagon train would grow a beaten path known as the Bozeman Trail.

Blood on the Ice

Red Cloud's Oglalas may have been oblivious of the knife edge on which they walked, but south of the Oregon Trail the Indian situation was obviously worsening. By the mid-1860s, the traditional buffalo ranges along the Republican River were already dwindling, not least because of the first white hunting parties converging from new settlements in Missouri, Kansas, and eastern Nebraska.

A solitary hunter equipped with an accurate large-bore Sharps rifle could fell up to 100 buffalo in a single outing. This new gun technology marked the beginning of a Plains-wide slaughter that within four decades would reduce an estimated 30 million animals to less than 1,000. It was the greatest mass destruction of warm-blooded animals in human history, far worse than what the world's whaling fleets had already accomplished, and as Sitting Bull was to lament years later, "A cold wind blew across the prairie when the last buffalo fell. A death wind for my people."

When whites killed the buffalo, the animals were skinned where they fell, everything but their hides and tongues—considered a delicacy—left to rot on the prairie. The hunters considered the rest of the meat worthless, but to the tribes this was not only a criminal physical waste, but a insult to the animals' spirits, to Mother Earth, to the Sacred Hoop of life itself.

For several years, the southern bands of the Cheyenne, Arapaho, and Lakota found themselves virtually fenced in by the Oregon Trail to the north and the Santa Fe Trail to the south. This territory was further constrained by a new branch of the Overland Stage that connected the East to the booming gold camps around Denver. With stations every twenty to twenty-five miles, a thin ribbon of American civilization spread across land promised to the Indians.

By the end of the Civil War, the southern tribes were forced to share even this tiny swath of territory with small regiments of buffalo hunters as well as stagecoach horses competing for pasturage. Among these put-upon Oglala bands were the Bear People and the followers of Spotted Tail.

By this time Spotted Tail was a changed man. Nine years earlier, he had been sentenced to twenty-four months of "imprisonment" at Fort Leavenworth for his part in the stagecoach robbery. Although he had actually spent most of that time working as an unpaid army scout, the sheer number of whites he encountered at the fort had transformed him. Fort Leavenworth was a steamboat hub on the Lower Missouri, and during those months he watched as thousands of well-armed Bluecoats passed through the territory. These were, he came to understand, just the tip of the American army's spear. At tribal councils and in private conversations during the seven years since his return, he had urged accommodation with the Americans, citing what one Minnesota Dakota had characterized as an enemy "as numerous as the leaves in the forest."

But Spotted Tail's voice was in the minority. By 1864, Indian raids on white travelers had become a regular occurrence.

The last straw for Washington was the defeat of a detachment of cavalry dispatched from Denver. Cheyenne Dog Soldiers ambushed the troop and beheaded the young lieutenant leading it. Rumors circulated that his head was later used in ball games at the Cheyenne camp. Upon hearing these rumors, the army general in charge of the Colorado Territory ordered a volunteer colonel, the Methodist minister John Chivington, to form a militia and run the hostiles to ground.

The army chose well. The forty-four-year-old Chivington was physically robust: he stood six feet five inches and carried his 260 pounds with the grace of an antelope. In his official portrait, his barrel chest seems about to burst from a blue tunic sporting two rows of shiny brass buttons. More to the point, Chivington hated Indians.

Chivington had been born in Ohio, and had spent time at tribal missionary posts in Kansas and Nebraska, where his low opinion of the Native inhabitants hardened. He exemplified a new breed of westerner, one who took a simple view: in any dispute, the Indian was wrong.

A magazine cover shows a man skinning a buffalo.
Library of Congress

Spotted Tail, two years younger than Red Cloud, was a Brule Sioux whose fierce opposition to white expansion across the Plains was broken by a two-year stint in a U.S. federal prison.
Courtesy National Anthropological Archives, Smithsonian Institution

Chivington operated with extraordinary freedom. The "Fighting Parson" instructed his Colorado volunteers that total war was the order of the day, every day. His detachments galloped along the South Platte and Republican, annihilating whatever small bands of Cheyenne, Arapaho, and Lakota they could catch. The unlucky Indians passing through these free-fire zones were usually the peaceable, the old, and the infirm. The more agile hostiles, mounted on fast ponies, were much too savvy to face Chivington's guns head-on.

White reprisals lessened during the summer of 1862, when Colonel Chivington's men were ordered south to head off a Confederate army advancing up from Texas through New Mexico. The Indians took advantage of the absence to form their largest war parties to date and to soak the Leavenworth–Denver turnpike with blood.

By the autumn of 1864, the split between the tribal militants and the pacifist faction had widened to a chasm. When, at the belated urging of Washington, Colorado's territorial governor offered sanctuary to any Indians "should they repair at once to the nearest military post," two Cheyenne bands struck out for Fort Lyon on the territory's southeastern plain. One was led by the chief Black Kettle, the other by White Antelope, and they were joined by a few followers of the Arapaho head man Left Hand. When they reached the fort in mid-autumn, they were ordered to surrender their weapons in exchange for daily food rations. By this time, Colonel Chivington had returned to Denver.

Fort Lyon's new commander, Major Edward Wynkoop, was a friend of Chivington's, and far less inclined than his predecessor toward distinguishing between hostile and friendly tribes. He looked for any excuse to declare Black Kettle and White Antelope hostiles, and when he found none he simply refused to give them food; returned their old muskets, bows, arrows, and knives; and ordered them off the premises. They were, he said, free to hunt in a limited territory bordering a stream called Sand Creek that fed into the Smoky Hill River about thirty-five miles northwest of the fort. The Cheyenne sensed a trap, but they were reassured that as long as Black Kettle flew the white flag of truce above his lodge next to an old American flag the head man had once received as a gift, no harm would come to them.

Two days after the Indians departed, on November 28, Chivington arrived at Fort Lyon with two field cannons and 700 volunteers. He took every precaution to keep his presence secret, throwing a ring of guards around the post to prevent anyone from leaving. That night he and the volunteers, and an additional 125 regular army troops, rode for Sand Creek.

At just past daybreak the next morning, they climbed a ridge overlooking the Indian camp. Most of the warriors were absent, hunting to the east. Of the 500 to 600 Indians remaining, more than half were sleeping women and children. Chivington ordered the Indian pony herd driven off. Then his howitzers erupted and the whites charged.

Black Kettle frantically raised the two flags over his tepee as his people fell around him—including White Antelope, whose death song was silenced by a bullet to the throat. It was a slaughter. The immediate survivors staggered to the nearby frozen creek bed, where women and children huddled beneath the high banks, and the few braves who were present gouged the earth with knives and tomahawks in an attempt to dig shooting pits. They were soon surrounded, and for more than two hours Chivington's volunteers picked them off like targets in a carnival game.

Afterward the colonel and his officers stood by as atrocities, such as severed limbs, ensued. Later, an investigative committee of the U.S. House of Representatives would report: "Barbarity of the most revolting character. Such, it is to be hoped, has never before disgraced the acts of men claiming to be civilized."

The soldiers departed at dusk—Chivington had lost ten men, with another thirty-eight wounded—and as night fell, the Indian survivors crawled out from beneath the dead. All told, close to 200 were murdered along Sand Creek that day, three quarters of them women and children. Those who escaped, Black Kettle among them, spent the next several days tramping across the frozen earth toward the warriors' hunting camp on the Smoky Hill. When they reached the site, one of his band's first acts was to banish Black Kettle and his family, who eventually moved to the country south of the Arkansas. Then the survivors plotted their revenge.

The Great Escape

Colonel Chivington's merciless attack at Sand Creek did more to unite the Plains tribes against the United States than any other incident in the long, bloody history of Indian–American relations. While the hills were still echoing with the wails of mourning mothers, wives, and daughters, Cheyenne runners with war pipes were sent out to the Lakota and the Arapaho. War councils convened across the territories, and in preparation for an unprecedented winter campaign, the head men of the three tribes selected nearly 1,000 braves to move on the closest army barracks.

These barracks were at Fort Rankin on the South Platte River in the northeast corner of Colorado. The Indians rode in formal battle columns, the Sioux warriors in the front. A place of honor was reserved for the once pacifist Spotted Tail.

At dawn on January 7, while the main body of warriors hid behind a row of rolling sand hills south of the fort, seven painted decoys descended from the snow-covered heights and paraded before the post. Predictably, a blend of cavalry and civilians poured out in pursuit. Before they could ride into the trap, some overanxious braves broke from concealment and charged.

The whites recognized the ambush, turned, and fled as cannons from the fort bombarded their pursuers. They reached the post, but not before losing fourteen cavalrymen and four civilians. The enraged head men ordered the offending braves quirted by the *akicita,* the ultimate humiliation, and led the war party one mile east to plunder the now abandoned stage station and warehouses at Julesburg.

Over the next month the southern Lakota, Cheyenne, and Arapaho cut a bloody swath through Kansas, Nebraska, and Colorado, finally circling back to again sack Julesburg, this time with the assistance of a party of northern Strong Hearts led by Crazy Horse. Again the garrison at Fort Rankin could do nothing but watch the (rebuilt) stock station burn.

But now the Indians recognized that time was running out. Although Colonel Chivington had resigned in the face of a pending court-martial, army troops from Denver, Nebraska's Fort Kearney, and Wyoming's Fort Laramie were already mobilizing. With certain retaliation awaiting them to the south, east, and west, there was no other direction for the southern tribes to ride but north into the Powder River Country. No soldiers would dare follow them into the great warrior chief Red Cloud's territory.

The combined tribal force of nearly 4,000 Indian men, women, and children rode in three loose parallel columns, with scouts fanned out to the front and on either side. They crossed the South Platte above Julesburg without incident. A few travelers reported spotting thousands of distant campfires, or hearing the beat of war drums for miles. Yet the army could not find them.

As they headed north, the Indians looted and burned farms, ranches, and stagecoach relay stations. Precious telegraph poles, hauled to the treeless prairie and pounded into the ground four years earlier, were hacked down; their wires were spooled and stolen. Supply wagons carrying food to Denver were stopped and destroyed, and the few late-starting emigrant wagon trains hoping to winter over at Fort Laramie were ransacked and torched.

When the Indian columns reached the Black Hills, the Arapaho broke off toward the southwest while the majority of Cheyenne and Lakota circled north of the range and rode for the Powder River. The exceptions were Spotted Tail and his band. The unpredictable Brule, having undergone yet another change of heart, vowed never again to fight the Americans, and took his people east to the White River, beneath the Badlands, where, aside from occasional treks to Fort Laramie, he would remain for the rest of his life.

The three columns had traversed more than 400 miles of bitter winter landscape, with the U.S. government having little idea of their whereabouts for most of the journey. They had also killed more soldiers, settlers, teamsters, and ranchers than the number of Cheyenne murdered at Sand Creek.

The new army commander of the region, General Grenville Dodge, ordered all-out war on all Indians, with no consideration given to geographic boundaries. Any Indian was fair game, and a deep hole dug beneath hastily erected gallows just beyond Fort Laramie's walls began to fill with corpses.

The southern tribes finally reached the Upper Powder in March 1865. They brought with them large herds of stolen cattle and packhorses, and travois piled high with looted sacks of flour, cornmeal, rice, sugar, and more. The northerners gathered goggle-eyed around strange bolts of multicolored cloth, and more than a few became nauseated after feasting on a mixture of tinned oysters, ketchup, and candied fruit.

But most alluring were the repeating rifles and ammunition taken from the torched ranches and mail stations. Red Cloud's warriors and most other fighters and hunters on the Upper Powder still relied primarily on bows and arrows, and the rush to trade for these new, prized weapons was loud and energetic.

It was initially a hesitant reunion, however, despite the air of excitement. There were many northern Oglalas, not least among them Red Cloud, who remembered well the insults that had fired the decades-long feud between the Smoke People and the Bear People. And though the Cheyenne had no such divisions, the years apart had worsened cultural differences between the northern and southern branches. The Northern Cheyenne, clad in rough buffalo robes and with red-painted buckskin strips braided through crow feathers entwined in their hair, barely recognized their southern cousins, who wore cloth leggings and wool serapes. The two branches even had some trouble communicating, as the Northern Cheyenne had adopted many words from the

Sioux dialect. In the end, however, turning away the ragged widows and bewildered orphans of Sand Creek would have been unthinkable.

Soon enough their dramatic stories set the Bad Faces' blood boiling. The southerners described the outrage at Sand Creek in all its wretched detail. Crazy Horse in particular was reported to have reacted to these tales of betrayal and brutality with an unconcealed rage and a call for blood vengeance.

Red Cloud saw that the white man's war had finally arrived on his doorstep. There was nowhere to run. Nor, he reasoned, should his people have to run. It was time, once and for all, to fight the mighty United States and expel the Americans from the High Plains. He had long planned how to do this. The only question had been when. Sand Creek had answered that: now.

War Council

In the early spring of 1865, not long after the southern tribes reached the Powder River Country, the leaders of the Sioux and Cheyenne convened a war council. With more than 2,000 braves at their disposal, Lakota war chiefs like Red Cloud, Hump, and Young Man Afraid of His Horses plotted strategy with Cheyenne war chiefs. These Cheyenne included Dull Knife and Roman Nose, who had both lost kinsmen at the Sand Creek massacre. Although each tribe kept its own laws and customs, all were gradually coming to think of themselves as "The People." They had the Americans to thank for that.

"The Great Spirit raised both the white man and the Indian," Red Cloud told his fellow fighters. "I think he raised the Indian first. He raised me in this land and it belongs to me. The white man was raised over the great waters, and his land is over there. Since they crossed the sea, I have given them room. There are now white people all about me. I have but a small spot of land left. The Great Spirit told me to keep it."

For once the squabbling bands and tribes were in agreement. They decided that after the spring buffalo hunt—which would be challenging, given the number of mouths to feed—the main force of the alliance would strike the Americans at the Bridge Station outpost. This was about 130 miles upstream from Fort Laramie. In the meantime, smaller groups of raiders who could be spared from the hunt were sent west, south, and east to keep the soldiers protecting the Glory Road and the South Pass of the Rockies off balance, while also gathering intelligence about the army's movements.

The plan was off to a rousing start in April when a war party of Cheyenne Dog Soldiers burned a key relay station west of Fort Laramie. The Indians killed all five of the station's defenders and staked their mutilated corpses to trees. The Dog Soldiers—along with Lakota riding under the leadership of Young Man Afraid of His Horses—next moved east and raided the outpost at Deer Creek. Through May and June they attacked Wyoming stage stations, wagon trains, and small army patrols, scalping and burning from Dry Creek to Sage Creek.

On one humiliating occasion, Americans troops that had been sent to chase down the Indians returned to Fort Laramie at dusk and reported no Indians within twenty-five miles of the post. They had no sooner unsaddled their horses on the parade ground than a band of about thirty Lakota galloped into the fort, shooting, yelling, and waving buffalo

C A N A D A

MONTANA

Yellowstone River

Bozeman Trail

Little
Bighorn
River

Powder River

Virginia City

Yellowstone Lake

Bighorn River

Bighorn Mountains

Fort
Phil
Kearny

IDAHO

WYOMING

Fort Laramie

Great Salt Lake

UTAH

COLORADO

Red Cloud's Territory at the Height of His Power, 1857-1868

Contemporary state names are shown.

```
0        50      100 miles
0   50  100  150 kilometers
```

Indian scouts on horseback. Their special skills included gathering clues from tracks, staying unseen while waiting, and following trails even in darkness. *Library of Congress*

robes. They stampeded the army mounts through the open gates. They were never caught.

The army had no idea when, where, or how the hostiles would strike next. But old frontier hands like Jim Bridger assured the officers that it was a long-held Indian custom to celebrate even the most minor victories with weeks of feasts. There was time, he said, to gather a large enough force to ride out and surprise them. But for once the mountain man was mistaken. Red Cloud was yet again one step ahead of his enemies.

23

Bloody Bridge Station

In 1859, the owner of a trading post on the south banks of the North Platte River built a 1,000-foot bridge across the river. Soon the government expanded this trading post into a sturdy fort constructed of lodgepole pine. Telegraph poles went up, and a company of cavalry was deployed to protect the new line.

It was Red Cloud's idea to attack this post, known as Bridge Station. He knew that its defeat and the destruction of the fort and bridge would halt settler traffic for months. Victory at Bridge Station would also allow the Indians an opportunity for further attacks against the smaller army camps that had sprouted along the Oregon Trail.

For most of that summer in 1865, the station had been manned by a feuding mix of Kansas and Ohio men, the Ohio men led by Lieutenant Caspar Collins. Collins had been known to ride off by himself along the Upper Powder, camping with friendly Oglalas and Brules. There were even reports that in less troubled times, Crazy Horse himself had taught Collins bits of the Lakota language as well as how to fashion a bow and arrows.

By all accounts Collins was a pleasant and capable junior officer. He had a good reputation among the enlisted men. In July, when a large company of Kansas cavalry arrived at Bridge Station, he was amused by their enthusiasm. "I never saw so many men so anxious in my life to have a fight with the Indians," Collins wrote in a letter home. "But ponies are faster than American horses, and I think they will be disappointed."

But there was bad blood between his Ohioans and the rough Kansas recruits. Not long after Collins was sent to Fort Laramie to secure fresh mounts, the commander of the new Kansas group banished most of the Ohio troops to a more isolated post farther west.

Collins returned to Bridge Station on the afternoon of July 25 to find only a small squad of his Ohio company. It was the very day Red Cloud chose to attack.

Earlier that morning, before Collins's arrival, the main body of Cheyenne and Lakota—which included Oglala, Brule, Miniconjou, Sans Arc, and Blackfoot Sioux warriors— had hidden themselves behind the red sandstone buttes on the north side of the river. Taking a lesson from the botched ambush at Fort Rankin, Red Cloud had raised a police force from Crazy Horse's Strong Hearts as insurance in case his excitable braves tried to break cover too early.

The Cheyenne recruited members of their own Crazy Dog Society to do the same. Red Cloud then sent a dozen or so riders in full battle regalia out into the little valley in front of the station, hoping to draw out most of its 119 defenders.

At first a howitzer battery seemed to take the bait, but after crossing the bridge the soldiers moved no farther, opting to dig in on the north bank of the river and lob shells into the hills. By this time, even the rawest recruit on the frontier was aware of the Indians' repeated use of a handful of braves to lay a trap. Collins had also been warned.

Red Cloud was restless but waited until dusk before signaling for the decoys to return. That night, he altered his plan and selected a small party of Bad Faces to creep beneath the north side of the bridge and hide themselves amid the brush and thick willows. At dawn he again deployed his baiting riders, who this morning cantered even closer to the fort and taunted the soldiers by shouting obscenities, in English, that they had learned from traders.

Again the ploy seemed to work. The gates opened, and at the head of a column of cavalry rode Lieutenant Collins.

But Red Cloud had no idea that the horsemen were not coming out to fight. They were planning on escorting into Bridge Station five army freight wagons returning from delivering supplies.

Earlier that morning as Collins had donned the new dress uniform that he had purchased at Fort Laramie, several of his remaining Ohioans had tried to discourage him from riding out with only twenty-eight men. When he persisted, they implored him to at least request from the Kansan commander a larger detail. Again Collins said no, and at this a fellow officer from his regiment handed him his own weapons, two

Colt revolvers. Collins stuck one into each boot, selected a high-strung gray horse from the stable, and mounted up at 7:30. Before departing, he handed his cap to his Ohio friend "to remember him by."

The Indian decoys scattered as Collins and his troop crossed the bridge, followed on foot by eleven soldiers acting as a volunteer rear guard. Those men watched from the riverbank as the riders moved half a mile into the North Platte Valley. The hills then erupted with painted warhorses, pinging arrows, and glinting steel.

The Lakota swept down from the northern buttes, and the Cheyenne rode in from the west. On Collins's orders, the little column wheeled into two lines and discharged a volley from their guns. A bitter-tasting fog of smoke rolled toward the river.

Then Collins flinched and nearly toppled from his horse. He had been shot in the hip, and a scarlet stain seeped through his pant leg. He was soon shot in the head with an arrow.

Indian and American horseflesh continued to collide at close quarters, the Indians slashing with knives and spears and swinging tomahawks and war clubs to avoid firing into their own lines. Cavalrymen fought back with revolvers. A galloping horse broke out of the smoky haze with a wounded trooper hunched over its neck, making for the bridge. Another followed. Then another. The rear guard of soldiers opened up, firing wildly into the fight.

As if by magic, the Bad Faces hidden beneath the bridge appeared. They threw their bodies in front of the retreating horsemen. The rear guard charged them, desperate to keep the escape route open. Riderless horses and single riders with arrows protruding from all parts of their bodies galloped back. A cannon boomed from the Bridge Station bastions, and soldiers on the catwalks watched an Indian drive his spear through the heart of a dismounted cavalryman, yank it out, turn, and lunge at another, piercing his chest. But the second soldier was not dead. He fell forward, pressed his revolver against his assailant's head, and with his last cartridge shot the Indian.

Thirty minutes into the fight, Red Cloud signaled the Cheyenne chief Roman Nose to move his Dog Soldiers. They thundered up the valley, approaching the freight wagons that Lt. Collins had planned on escorting. The train's five lead scouts, cresting a rise in the road that put them in sight of the fort, saw a horde of 500 Indians bearing down on them. The scouts galloped for the river and splashed their mounts into the current. Three made it across.

The men at the bridge who had formed the rear guard, including the lieutenant who had given Collins his revolvers, retreated to the stockade. The lieutenant volunteered to lead a rescue, reminding the post commander that the twenty wagoneers were also men from the 11th Ohio Cavalry. The Kansan refused, insisting that he needed every available body to defend the fort. The lieutenant punched him in the face, was subdued and arrested, and was taken to the guardhouse at about the time Roman Nose descended on the supply wagons just reaching the ridgeline at the same time as the scouts.

The Ohio teamsters recognized that it was suicide to try

to burst through so many hostiles. They made for a shallow hollow between the road and the North Platte. They formed the best corral possible with their five wagons and a few empty wooden chests, and attempted to hobble their thirty mules. But an Indian captured the bell mare and led her off, the rest of the animals following. With her went their last chance of escape.

Night fell and the Lakota and Cheyenne returned to the hills, while the post commander at Bridge Station counted twenty-eight men missing and presumed dead, with twice as many wounded. The telegraph lines east of the fort had been cut, and at ten o'clock a scout mounted a captured Indian pony and slipped through a side gate with instructions to ride for Deer Creek Station twenty-eight miles to the east. From there, word of the attack could be transmitted to Gen. Patrick Connor, the new commander, at Fort Laramie. The scout made it through.

On the far side of the red bluffs, the day ended just as inconclusively for Red Cloud. There is no record of his losses, but the army estimated that sixty Indians had fallen. Though this number was probably inflated, it was still a significant toll. Moreover, not only had the Native force failed to take the outpost, but a good number of Collins's cavalry had managed to make their way back through the Bad Faces and across the bridge to safety.

The Cheyenne Dog Soldiers blamed the Lakota, a few even insinuating that the Lakota were cowards. The Lakota moved for their weapons but were held back at the last moment by order of the frustrated Red Cloud.

Red Cloud and Roman Nose spent the night repairing the damaged alliance, and the next morning the great war party paraded before Bridge Station just beyond cannon range, then swung back into the hills and vanished. Red Cloud recognized that despite his superior numbers, most of his fighters were far too inexperienced and ill-disciplined. Even more disturbing was the way the tribes had nearly turned on one another. The best he could hope for was that as the war progressed, his followers would learn.

24

The Hunt for Red Cloud

When the Civil War ended in April 1865, the battered U.S. Army began replacing the under-qualified state militias patrolling the West with more experienced troops. South of the Arkansas River, their orders were to eliminate the Kiowa and the Comanche, who were blocking movement along the Santa Fe Trail into New Mexico.

North of the Platte River, they were to kill Red Cloud and Sitting Bull.

General Ulysses S. Grant, the army's commander in chief, had long planned for such a moment. The previous November, the day after the Sand Creek massacre, Grant called on Major General John Pope to lead a division of soldiers in the summer of 1865 to ensure the safety of the trail stamped out by John Bozeman.

Gen. Pope appointed the vicious Gen. Dodge as his number two in charge. Together they decided on a plan to crush the High Plains tribes with a large-scale pincer movement.

Portrait of Maj. Gen. John Pope.
Library of Congress

Gen. Connor's forces would march north out of Fort Laramie to face Red Cloud, while Gen. Sully—the same officer who had stuck the heads of dead Indians on poles as a warning—would lead a column northwest from Sioux City to finally finish off Sitting Bull. Sully's cavalry had already been fighting Sitting Bull for two years. The ideal time for a renewed assault was early spring, before the lush summer prairie grasses allowed the Indian ponies to regain their speed and stamina.

But additional troops were not assigned to Pope's new division until midsummer. The majority of the volunteers ordered into Indian country from Civil War battlefields felt as if they had fulfilled their duty to the Union. They slowly marched west in hopes that their discharge papers would beat them to their new post so that they would not have to fight any longer. Many of those hopes were realized, and nearly half of the 4,500 reinforcements never made it.

Connor may have wished the same for the rest. One regiment of 600 Kansas cavalry rode into Fort Laramie and promptly mutinied, refusing to ride any farther. This forced Connor to aim weapons on their camp to bring them under control. Still, he was confident that the 2,500 additional men he had received—including the Kansas mutineers— were more than enough to merge with Sully and defeat Red Cloud, Sitting Bull, and whatever allies had been foolish enough to join them.

In June 1865, Connor issued his infamous order: find the hostile tribes and kill all the males over the age of twelve.

The plan faltered from the start. Rivers and streams were still swollen from heavy spring rains. This delayed Sully's Missouri crossing for weeks. When Sully finally managed to ferry his 1,200 troopers across the river, they rode up and down its banks and tributaries for nearly a month without finding Sitting Bull. Not finding Indians was becoming routine for the army across the frontier.

Finally, Sully's force was pulled back to Minnesota when the War Department overreacted to a raid by a small party of Dakota Sioux near Mankato. He and his men were ordered to remain in the state. At faraway Fort Laramie, Connor was forced to readjust on the run.

In early July, Connor ordered nearly 1,400 Michigan volunteers under the command of Colonel Nelson Cole to ride until they met and united with the regiment of Kansas cavalry sent out from Fort Laramie. This combined troop would create a border around Red Cloud's multi-tribal forces, which Connor was confident he would locate near their favorite hunting grounds on the Upper Powder River. Connor, meanwhile, would ride at the head of 1,000 men up John Bozeman's trail, and all three American columns were to converge on Rosebud Creek, the heart of Red Cloud's territory.

It was fine as a tactical approach on paper. On the ground, however, it failed utterly. The sulky Kansans' movement proved almost worthless, and the grain-fed army horses in Cole's command withered and broke down on the dried-out South Dakota prairie.

Although three columns of infantry and cavalry were

snaking across the High Plains searching for Red Cloud, he appeared to have no idea that he was the object of such a hunt. He spent his days at leisure, and whiled away long nights attending formal medicine ceremonies, feasts, and scalp dances where he, Young Man Afraid of His Horses, and Roman Nose were given places of honor.

In an attempt at great unity, Red Cloud sent Bad Face representatives down to take part in Sitting Bull's large Sun Dance. The Hunkpapa chief failed to reciprocate, and this insult was the beginning of a lifelong rift between Red Cloud and Sitting Bull.

Toward mid-August, a Lakota hunting party spotted a civilian wagon train escorted by a company of cavalry traveling west near the South Dakota Badlands. Red Cloud and Dull Knife roused 500 warriors to ride out against the party. Before reaching the wagon train, they captured and killed one of its scouts. They then spread across two mesas flanking a narrow valley and waited for the whites to enter. When the wagon train appeared, the Indians began taking potshots from the high ground, whooping and taunting the whites all the while. The Bluecoat escort responded with howitzer fire that fell harmlessly, merely gouging chunks of earth from the surrounding hills.

Soon a white flag went up; the whites wanted a conference. Red Cloud and Dull Knife rode out to meet with the expedition's two leaders, the civilian wagon master and an army captain.

Incredibly, the two chiefs promised the train safe passage on the condition that the group travel north of the Powder

River buffalo grounds as well as give them a wagonload of sugar, coffee, flour, and tobacco as a toll.

This may seem a curious decision for warriors who only weeks earlier had vowed to drive all whites from their territory. The explanation lay in the fact that the Indian and white man did not adhere to the same concept of warfare. The Sioux and Cheyenne viewed the Americans as a more numerous, better-armed version of the Crows, Shoshones, or Pawnee. Unlike invading soldiers, a trespassing emigrant train, even one escorted by cavalry, was more of a nuisance than a threat.

Although a few Lakota in closer contact with the whites were dimly aware of how much carnage the Americans had inflicted on one another during the Civil War, most had no grasp of the white man's concept of battle as a year-round endeavor. The Indians considered that the skirmish at Bridge Station had been a victory and Sand Creek had been avenged. Now it was natural to fall back, plan for the autumn buffalo hunt, and settle into winter camps to await next year's fighting season. There was even a thought that the lesson of Bridge Station might induce the whites to abandon the Powder River Country altogether.

As it was, Connor's two flanking columns finally met, almost a hundred miles away from their planned juncture. Unknowingly, Col. Cole proceeded to march his 2,000 men directly between Sitting Bull's Hunkpapa village on the Little Missouri and the Lakota-Cheyenne force camped on the Powder River. Cole sent out riders to find Connor's column. They returned exhausted and bewildered.

Connor dispatched his scouts to find Cole. They could not. The Americans were, in effect, lost in the wilderness; they were running low on supplies; and the still grumbling Kansas contingent was ready to desert at any moment.

This is how Sitting Bull and his braves found them.

Burn the Bodies;
Eat the Horses

When Sitting Bull's scouts spied the billowing dust clouds of Colonel Cole's force not far from where the Powder River empties into the Yellowstone, he and his frustrated Hunkpapas roared out of camp.

Cole's force outnumbered the attackers by four to one, but his men and their horses were weakened after marching for weeks through the heat of a baking drought. Their skin was cracked, and a fine dusting of yellow soil coated their lips and tongues. So instead of counterattacking, at the first sign of the Sioux, Col. Cole ordered his troop to assume a defensive position, corralling up near a grove of leafy scrub oak. Through four days and nights the Sioux probed, running off a few horses and wagon mules. Sitting Bull personally captured one officer's majestic black stallion. But the Indians could neither penetrate the makeshift battlements nor lure out the Americans.

Then nature intervened. On the first day of September,

the temperature dropped seventy degrees and a freak blizzard swept down from the north. More than 200 of the Americans' weakened horses died. After burning his now useless wagons, harnesses, and saddles, Cole had no choice but to march his men up the Powder River.

Sitting Bull had sent out messengers to Red Cloud's camp, and his Hunkpapas and Dakotas were now reinforced by small parties of Oglalas as well as some Miniconjous and Sans Arcs. These Sioux kept up a steady harassment of the slow-moving Americans.

The farther southeast the troop drove, the more concerned Sitting Bull became about straying too far from his defenseless village back on the Little Missouri River. His scouts informed him that General Sully had pulled back across the Missouri into Minnesota, but one never knew. The Hunkpapas harassed the column for two more days, and then fell off to ride home.

It was now Red Cloud's turn.

On September 5, the Bad Faces leader assembled 2,000 braves to meet the beleaguered American force. As his battleground, he chose a bend in the Powder River marked by tall, sheer sandstone bluffs broken by winding ravines. It was an ideal site for an ambush.

Red Cloud, however, did not ride with the war party that day. Some historians believe that after days of fasting and mind-cleansing vision quests, the Cheyenne chief Roman Nose begged for the honor of leading the combined Sioux-Cheyenne force. Red Cloud apparently granted Roman Nose that honor, and to represent the Lakota he sent

Stereoscopic view of Cheyenne chief Roman Nose, 1865. *The New York Public Library*

Crazy Horse and Young Man Afraid of His Horses.

Without the Oglala head man present, the Indians reverted to their age-old battle tactics. Instead of ambushing the troopers from the rocky ridges, or even surprising them head-on, warriors broke into small groups according to their soldier societies, intent on stealing horses and counting coup.

Some had wonderful luck. A group of Cheyenne led by Roman Nose chased a company of cavalry into a thicket of cottonwood trees banking the north side of the Powder River. The Indians dismounted and, using the thick leaf cover, crept in after them. Near the riverbank they broke into a clearing, where they found eighty saddled mounts tied to the bushes. Across the river the fleeing cavalrymen emerged, dripping wet. None had fired a shot.

Lifted by this small victory, Roman Nose attempted to rally his attackers into a coherent battle group. By this time, the main body of Col. Cole's troops had formed its wagons into a hollow square, its rear against the high hills.

The combined tribal force charged the corral en masse. They were repelled by gunfire. As a smoky dusk fell over the battlefield, the Indians predictably grew tired of the standoff. The Cheyenne were the first to depart, riding off to strike camp and move east toward the Black Hills in preparation for the fall buffalo hunt. Cole took advantage of this to set his troops on the move. He drove southwest as a few Sioux continued to trail him, intent mainly on stealing horses. But the opportunity for a showdown had passed.

Three days later Cole's Pawnee scouts, followed by a platoon of cavalry, nearly stumbled into the eastern edge of Red

Cloud's huge camp. A band of Cheyenne, one of the last to depart for winter camp in the east, saw the scouts. But the scouts were so distant that the Cheyenne thought they were either Lakota or Arapaho returning from the fight with the soldiers, and paid them no attention. The scouts retreated and hid on top of a steep cutback, allowing the now moving Cheyenne to pass. Then the cavalry ambushed the Cheyenne and killed every one.

When a messenger reported the situation to Cole, the colonel understood that for once he had the element of surprise. He took the offensive, organizing his troop into a full frontal charge.

Red Cloud was unprepared for the surprise attack. With his force depleted by the departure of the Cheyenne who had afterward been ambushed, he organized a frantic holding action. Women and girls raced to dismantle houses, called lodges, as teenage herders rounded up ponies from the surrounding grasslands. The scene at the center of the Indian camp resembled a rodeo, with armed braves lassoing and mounting any horse available. It would not be enough.

Then, suddenly, as if summoned by the *Wakan Tanka* itself, the weather again intervened on the Indians' behalf. The sky to the west darkened as billowing thunderheads growled down from the Bighorns. A driving sleet pounded the prairie for the next thirty-six hours, ending the fight. The Indians slipped away in the dim light, and the American soldiers lost another 400 horses and mules to the bitter cold.

When the storm broke on September 9, the dazed Americans again burned the last of their expendable supplies, including their wagons. Col. Cole's remaining animals were too weak and his men too exhausted to continue carrying the dead, and he ordered the corpses thrown onto the fires to spare them mutilation.

He then led what remained of his ragtag troop southwest up the Powder River valley. Such was their condition when Gen. Connor's scouts, led by Jim Bridger, found their camp.

No one was happier to gaze upon Bridger's leathery face that cold, dreary day in September 1865 than Col. Cole and his starving troop. Bridger told Cole that Gen. Connor's column was only sixty miles away. A short distance beyond Connor, he said, was a new fort stocked with abundant supplies. It was enough to give a jaunty step to Cole's men, who reached the rectangular log structure in late September.

All told, the summer campaign of 1865 had been a disaster. The U.S. Army spent the fighting season scouring the High Plains for hostiles and came away with nothing to show for it besides a record of bad judgment, poor discipline, and failure.

The confused campaign to crush Red Cloud left Gen. Connor too disgusted to even request written reports from his subordinates, and he worded his own dispatch to Gen. Dodge as vaguely as possible. He minimized the number of army casualties—stating that there had been between twenty and fifty—and inflated Indian losses to nearly absurd proportions, estimating between 200 and 500 killed or wounded.

Meanwhile one of his own junior officers admitted, "I cannot say as we killed one." Gen. Connor made no mention of the large herds of army mules and big American horses now mingling with Indian ponies in winter camps, nor of the surly mood of his volunteers who finally staggered back into Fort Laramie in October—their uniforms so tattered that they reminded one officer of a line of "tramps."

Gen. Dodge continued the charade. In his own report to his superior officer, Gen. Pope, he described the expedition as a wild success. He also wrote that the small, new fort the army had established farther north—which he had named Camp Connor—was now outfitted with a skeleton company. This meant that the United States had finally established a foothold in the heart of the Powder River Country.

Gen. Dodge, however, was forced to make one concession, suggesting that the Union Pacific Railroad might be better laid nearer to the South Platte than to Red Cloud's domain. Other than this, Dodge concluded, all that was needed to grind down the aggressive northern tribes once and for all and to open the Bozeman Trail was more time, funds, and military equipment.

But Washington had lost its faith. Gen. Dodge's requests for more troops and supplies were costing the government $24 million annually—$3.2 billion in today's currency—and this money might be better spent on Reconstruction, the plan to unify the country and fix the economy after the Civil War. The government saw no alternative but to fall back on a tried-and-true stratagem to deal with the prairie. The United States, Congress decided, would offer the High Plains Indians a new treaty.

PART FOUR

The War

Memory is like riding a trail at night with a lighted torch. The torch casts its light only so far, and beyond that is darkness. —*Ancient Lakota saying*

26

War Is Peace

In the fall of 1865, Indian agents approached bands of Hunkpapas, Yanktonais, Blackfoot Sioux, Yanktons, Sans Arcs, Two Kettles, and Brules living near the Missouri River with a blunt message: the raids on emigrants and settlers must cease, and a war against the United States would be unwise. But America was not heartless, the agents added, and in exchange for acceptance of Washington's latest peace offer, they promised the Indians acreage, farm tools and seed, and protection against any tribes who took exception to these new agricultural pursuits.

The Sioux were naturally resistant. Living in houses, tilling fields, sending their children to school—these were the white man's values and principles. But the agents, aware that the Upper Missouri tribes had suffered the most from the alarming thinning of the buffalo herds, reminded the Indians that the fifteen-year annuity payments from the Horse Creek Treaty were about to expire. They offered a

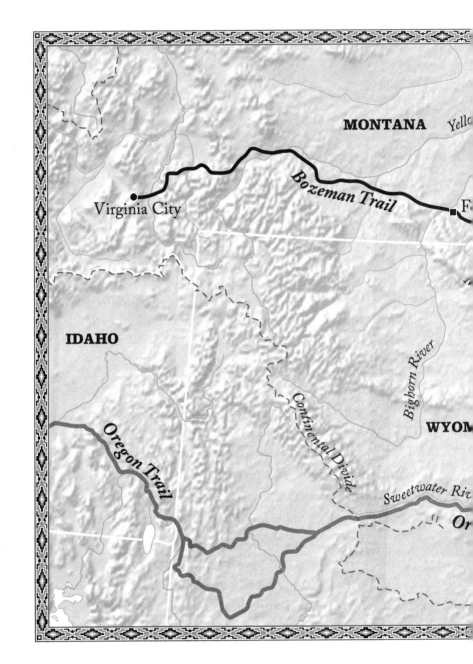

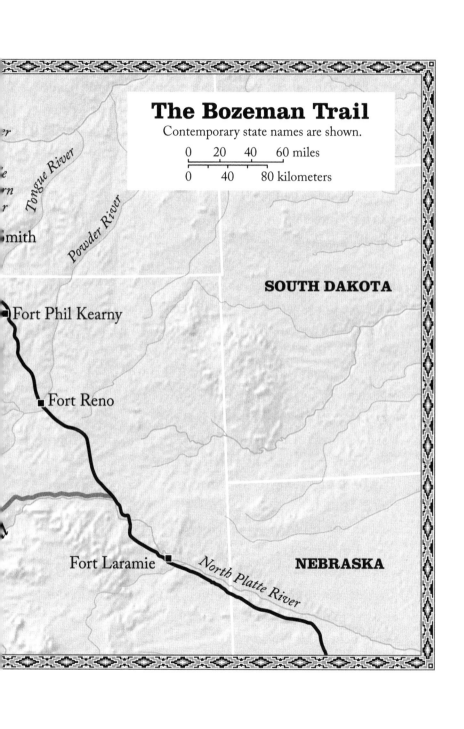

The Bozeman Trail

Contemporary state names are shown.

```
0    20    40    60 miles
0        40      80 kilometers
```

Tongue River

Powder River

...mith

SOUTH DAKOTA

Fort Phil Kearny

Fort Reno

Fort Laramie

NEBRASKA

North Platte River

solution: a new, twenty-year deal at increased rates.

All the United States asked in return was that the bands move permanently away from the trails and roads leading west, and vow not to bother the whites defiling their old lands with mechanical reapers, threshing machines, and barbed wire. It was a stunning demonstration of the Indians' desperation that by October the Lakota Sioux agreed to the treaty in a ceremony at Fort Sully, located at the mouth of the Cheyenne River.

Newspaper headlines declared peace with the Sioux. Eastern reporters and editors, unaware that "the Sioux" came in many variations, wrote that the Bozeman Trail was now safe for travel. The government believed that a similar pact could be signed with Red Cloud and his followers. Indian agents sent runners into the Powder River Country to announce that come spring, the United States would be willing to offer even better terms in the form of exclusive rights to the game-laden territory lying between the Black Hills, the Bighorn Mountains, and the Yellowstone River in exchange for the right of passage along the Bozeman Trail. There was no mention of farming.

The message from Washington was clear: avoid war at all costs. A war-weary America did not want any further conflict, particularly with Indians. And vocal religious groups, such as the Quakers, turned their attention from the emancipation of slaves to the justice and wisdom of America's treatment of the western tribes.

But the real reason for a shift in Indian policy was money. Eastern politicians were pressured by taxpayers tired of supporting the expensive Frontier Army when the costly task of Reconstruction was only beginning. Several congressional commissions formed to study the "Indian problem." The members of these committees tended to be both self-serving and naive. Grandstanding senators and congressmen began to personally conduct "fact-finding" missions to the West. Sand Creek was a favorite stopover for photo opportunities.

These politicians were in for a surprise. The westerners—whose numbers were still sparse—had no sympathy for the "savages." Despite local feeling, Washington was determined to reach some sort of compromise with the High Plains tribes—a clean, simple solution to avoid further bloodshed and expense.

Big Bellies and Shirt Wearers

In the autumn of 1865, Lakota head men and warriors were convening in the foothills of the Bighorn Mountains, seventy miles northwest of Fort Laramie. They wanted to revive a decades-old system of governance.

This system called for seven veteran chiefs to act as an advisory war council for the tribe, concentrating on battle tactics and strategy. On the banks of an unnamed creek over a feast of buffalo tongue and boiled dog, Red Cloud was selected as the "first among equals" of these *Tezi Tanka,* or "Big Bellies"—the wise heads who would guide the tribes through what all believed was inevitable war with the whites.

At the Big Belly assembly, Red Cloud officially declared the 1865 fighting season over. The Lakota agreed to reassemble for a war council in the spring. Perhaps they would even accept the white man's invitation to come to Fort Laramie for treaty talks. After all, Red Cloud reasoned, what better way to size up an enemy than to meet him in person?

Before the gathering disbanded, however, he and the six other Big Bellies chose four young men to act as ceremonial "Shirt Wearers" who would keep discipline among the braves and lead the war parties into battle. Among these were Young Man Afraid of His Horses and Crazy Horse. Red Cloud had begun to take a serious interest in Crazy Horse, the pale young warrior with an indefinable spirit.

Now twenty-five, Crazy Horse was slender and sinewy, and his lightness of posture often left the impression that he was smaller than his five feet nine inches. His ethereal quality was enhanced by his wavy hair, now waist length and usually worn in two braids that framed his narrow face and his unusually delicate nose, which observers described variously as "straight and thin" and "sharp and aquiline." Whites who met him over the years were usually struck most by his penetrating hazel eyes.

The land of Red Cloud's and Crazy Horse's youth was changing. Droughts lasted longer, grasslands had become more sparse, and even the resilient wild mustang herds, like the buffalo herds, appeared to be thinning.

Yet the Powder River Basin, because of its location between two mountain ranges and its many bountiful rivers, escaped the environmental troubles affecting vast portions of the West. Game proliferated in the area, cool breezes still wafted down from the mountains, and lush sweet grass scented the air. All of Red Cloud's plans were of a single piece—to close down the pathway into his people's verdant country, forever. He saw the world in primary colors, and if need be, he would paint John Bozeman's trail blood red.

Colonel Carrington's Overland Circus

"The pending treaty between the United States and the Sioux Indians at Fort Laramie renders it the duty of every soldier to treat all Indians with kindness. Every Indian who is wronged will visit his vengeance upon *any* white man he may meet."

Colonel Henry Beebee Carrington wrote these words on June 13, 1866, as he rode west with his family and a battalion of soldiers. He was still in eastern Nebraska and had yet to meet a hostile Indian, so he could not possibly have known how right he was.

Carrington was posted to Fort Laramie and in charge of 220 men of the 2nd Battalion of the 18th Infantry Regiment. His task was to protect the Bozeman Trail and construct a string of forts through the heart of the Powder River Country. The battalion that set out from Ohio was already undermanned by 700 soldiers.

· · ·

Col. Henry Beebee Carrington.
Library of Congress

William Judd Fetterman had long desired military service. Born in 1835 into a Connecticut military family, William did not know his mother, who died from complications during childbirth, and was orphaned at nine years old with the death of his father, Lt. George Fetterman. He went to live with his uncle William Bethel Judd, another regular army officer, who served with distinction during the Mexican War.

Judd, like George Fetterman, had graduated from West Point, and the young William Fetterman hoped to follow in their footsteps. But when he applied to the military academy in 1853, he was rejected by the admissions board for unknown reasons. The eighteen-year-old grudgingly took up a career in banking, working in Rochester, New York, before moving to Delaware. In 1861, a second opportunity for military service arose with the expansion of the Union Army at the outbreak of the Civil War. Fetterman, now twenty-six, jumped at the chance.

Fetterman became a first lieutenant less than two months after the rebels attacked Fort Sumter. In June 1861 he reported for duty at Camp Thomas in Columbus, Ohio. The depot was under the command of another civilian who had volunteered for service, abolitionist attorney Col. Henry Beebee Carrington. Fetterman arrived in Columbus just five days after Carrington, and together the two officers spent the next five months organizing and training the companies of raw volunteers.

It was soon apparent that the physically frail Carrington's greatest assets were political and clerical. Fetterman, on the other hand, seemed a born field commander. Carrington and

Fetterman seemed to sense that they complemented each other, and their combined skills were necessary to turn the regiment into a trim, well-disciplined unit. They also became personal friends.

Carrington's knack for recruiting kept him in charge of training depots in Ohio and, later, Indiana, while Fetterman, serving on the battlefield under General William Tecumseh Sherman, was promoted to battalion commander.

Following the end of the Civil War, Carrington and Capt. William Judd Fetterman decided to make the army their career.

By the spring of 1866, both Carrington and the Union Pacific Railroad tracks had reached as far west as Fort Kearney, Nebraska. Col. Carrington was elated when boxcars arrived, hauling not only reinforcements for his battalion, but also pallets full of supplies. He was also surprised to find that Gen. William Tecumseh Sherman, whom President Grant had installed as the military commander of the entire western United States, was riding along, making his first inspection trip to the frontier.

In late May 1866, Carrington and his battalion departed Fort Kearney. Over 1,000 men—700 soldiers, 11 officers, and several hundred civilian teamsters driving more than 200 wagons—followed the well-worn Oregon Trail. The infantrymen marched in the front, followed by the wagons, and then at least 700 beef cattle herded by mounted officers and foot soldiers. Someone dubbed the long train "Carrington's Overland Circus," and though it is not recorded who coined the phrase, suspicion naturally fell on the sixty-two-year-old Jim Bridger, the expedition's chief scout.

The troopers could hardly ignore the Indians watching them from every butte and mesa. At first, Bridger assured the soldiers that they were friendly. But when the column approached a rundown army post known as Camp Cottonwood midway between Fort Kearney and Julesburg, the old trapper's demeanor changed. He rose each morning before the reveille bugle, downed a few bites of pemmican, and brewed a pot of bitter coffee over a smoldering pile of buffalo chips. He would then confer in Carrington's tent before disappearing into the vastness. No one would see him again until dusk, when he would return to give the colonel a report.

One morning, a Brule head man rode into camp. Carrington greeted him with military courtesy, and with one of Bridger's scouts interpreting, the two parleyed over coffee and a pipe. The Brule told the colonel that many Lakota bands were camped near Fort Laramie, led by chiefs who were willing to listen to the white negotiators.

With his Bozeman Trail mapping mission in mind, Carrington asked the Indian for geographic information on the Powder River Country. The Brule ignored the question and said, "The fighting men in that country . . . They will not give you the road unless you whip them."

Thereafter, the "Circus" wagons were drawn into tight, interlocking squares each night. As a further precaution, Carrington issued orders bringing in mounted officers who had fallen into the habit of riding out at the sight of game.

Two weeks out of Fort Kearney, the column reached

Julesburg. They had to float their gear on makeshift ferries across the mile-wide Platte River running high with snow-melt. The men then veered northwest, following the north fork of the river.

A week later, with the temperature above a hundred degrees and a rising wind ripping the canvas covers from his freight wagons, Col. Carrington crested a cactus-studded ridge overlooking the gates of Fort Laramie. The searing heat had turned most of the prairie brown, and across the dusty flats were camped more than 2,000 Lakota, Cheyenne, and Arapaho "in assorted sizes, sexes and conditions; dressed, half dressed and undressed."

Col. Carrington scanned what he called the "menagerie" through his binoculars and was shocked by the lax security. There were no sentries posted around the fort, and Indians and soldiers mingled freely inside the stockade. He decided to temporarily camp his raw troops some distance away to avoid accidental misunderstandings.

That evening, Carrington splashed across the shallow Laramie River and entered the fort. He introduced himself to its commander, who was serving as a member of the government's peace commission. He met the civilian negotiators, including a superintendent of the Office of Indian Affairs who was to chair the next day's treaty ceremonies.

The colonel was also introduced to several Lakota head men. They had learned of his mission from the Brules who had visited him, and they were cold toward the "Little White Chief." The terms of the treaty to allow Americans passage through the Powder River Country had not even been laid out or discussed—and already the white soldiers presumed to ride north and build forts? Carrington understood that it would be hard to dispute this point, but he intended to try nonetheless.

The following morning, the superintendent from the Office of Indian Affairs pulled Col. Carrington aside. He assured Carrington that nearly all of the Brule, Miniconjou, and Oglala chiefs in attendance were ready to sign the treaty. Only a few from the Upper Powder were holding out and still needed to be convinced. But they were already in camp, and the superintendent had no doubt that they would come around. Carrington asked who these holdouts were. The superintendent rattled off a few names: Young Man Afraid of His Horses, Spotted Tail, Red Cloud. The latter two, Col. Carrington was told, "rule the [Lakota] nation."

This information was half right. By now the name Red Cloud was familiar to every soldier west of the Missouri. Although he was technically outranked in the Oglala hierarchy by Old Man Afraid of His Horses in time of peace, this was not such a time. According to Col. Carrington's account, the Indian agents had made great efforts to secure the Bad Face war chief's attendance by showing more deference to him than to any other Indian. They were unaware that Red Cloud had planned to be there all along in order to take the measure of his enemies.

Here Be Monsters

Col. Carrington and his men pushed off from Fort Laramie on June 17, 1866, the day before the peace conference formally ended. The conference was "a disgusting farce and disgraceful swindle," according to J. B. Weston, an attorney who witnessed the ceremony.

Weston's analysis contradicted the official report of the Indian Affairs superintendent, who wrote to Washington, "Satisfactory treaty concluded with the Sioux. . . . Most cordial feeling prevails."

Some head men, weary of constant war, had "signed the treaty" by touching the pen—that is, placing their fingers on a fountain pen held by an army adjutant over their names. They included most of the southern Lakota, the Bear People from the Republican River corridor, as well as Spotted Tail, who had ridden down from his territory south of the Black Hills to also agree to the terms. But most ominously, none of the bolder chiefs had done so.

In fact, during the treaty negotiations, Young Man Afraid of His Horses had warned Col. Carrington that if he dared lead his troops into the Powder River Country, "in two moons the command would not have a hoof left."

After Young Man Afraid of His Horses made his threat, Red Cloud had risen as the conclave fell silent. "The Great Father sends us presents and wants a new road," Red Cloud said through an interpreter. "But the White Chief already goes with soldiers to steal the road before the Indian says yes or no."

Now the great head man's voice rose to a shout. "I will talk with you no more. I will go now, and I will fight you. As long as I live, I will fight you for the last hunting grounds."

With that, Red Cloud, Young Man Afraid of His Horses, and several other Lakota leaders stormed out of the fort, saddled their horses, and galloped north. They were joined by many warriors from bands whose leaders had touched the pen.

Red Cloud's speech was still ringing in Col. Carrington's ears as he and his battalion set out several days later for the Powder River Country. It was 150 miles to the old Camp Connor, which had been renamed Fort Reno, and beyond that the world as the white soldiers knew it would end. The journey through this edge of the American empire would provide Carrington and his men with a greater understanding of just what they were to face in the months ahead.

The trail to Fort Reno, thick with prickly pear and saltbush, was punctuated by but a few lonely trading posts and ferry crossings. The troop was watched the entire length of the march by Lakota blending into the willows in shady hollows or, concealed beneath wolf skins, lying on high rim rock. Jim Bridger, who picked up Indian signs each day, reported to Carrington, "They follow ye always. They've seen ye, every day. And when ye don't see any of them about, is just the time to look for their devilment."

The first glimpse of Fort Reno was sobering. Set on a small rise blanketed with thistle and greasewood, it overlooked a maze of arroyos and low washes, the cracked-mud beds ideal for concealing Indian raiding parties.

The outpost was a rotting, weatherworn log structure plugged with mud; a dilapidated corral adjoined a string of warehouses built into low, red shale hills. Few men or officers from the battalion had ever seen a frontier post constructed to repel a full frontal Indian attack. This one was dominated by two defensive bastions holding two of the post's six mountain howitzers, and rifle loopholes had been bored through the adobe walls to accommodate shooting. The place struck the soldiers more as a prison than a military installation.

Col. Carrington had originally planned to demolish Fort Reno and transport any salvageable food and construction supplies to a site closer to the Black Hills with better access to wood, water, and pasturage. But eleven hard days on the road had changed his mind. Both soldiers and civilian travelers would need a secure post where they could lay over as they traversed the Bozeman Trail, and even if the unimpressive pile of wood 150 miles from Fort Laramie did not deserve the name "fort," it could certainly serve as a way station.

Reno Station was thus born as a midway stopover for

resting tired stock and repairing broken wagons between the Oregon Trail and the new posts Carrington intended to build farther north. He relieved the weary troops who had wintered over at Reno Station, and then selected a company of sixty to seventy men from his own battalion to permanently man the structure. Then he and his officers set out to explore their new possession.

The warehouses had been inundated by the winter's terrible snows, and the thick slabs of bacon stocked within were so rotten that gobs of greenish, slimy fat were falling off the meat. An infestation of mice had burrowed a network of tunnels through the flour sacks, whose contents had caked around the droppings and dead rodents. The men improvised a large sieve out of burlap sacks to separate the dead mice and the larger pieces of excrement. What remained of this unappetizing mess was repackaged and loaded onto wagons.

Carrington was further astonished to learn that three emigrant trains bound for Montana were camped a few hundred yards away over a nearby ridge, awaiting a military escort up the Bozeman Trail. A fourth train, he was told, had already departed.

When he rode out to meet the travelers the following morning, he was appalled. A blinding summer hailstorm—the stones as large as eggs, one trooper recorded in his journal—had transformed the camps into mud pigpens, and none of the expeditions' leaders had taken any precaution against Indian raids. The wagons were spread haphazardly across a gorgeous valley flecked with wild rose and pink wintergreen, and the mules and horses roamed free. When Carrington gently chided one wagon master for his lax security, the man scoffed at him: "We'll never see an Indian unless they come to beg for sugar, flour, or tobacco."

On the ride back to Reno Station, Carrington began formulating a set of regulations to be issued to all civilian trains passing up the Bozeman Trail. Vital in his mind was instilling a sense of discipline in these wild, independent-minded travelers.

No trains with fewer than thirty armed men, he decided, would be allowed to move forward. (The number would soon be revised upward, to forty.) And each passenger on any train that did meet this quota would have to sign in at every fort along the route. If a traveler was signed in at one post but failed to appear with the train at the next, the train could not go on until the straggler caught up. This, Carrington hoped, would not only end "the constant separation and scattering of trains pretending to act in concert," but also eliminate the Indians' most tempting targets.

That same afternoon, Carrington dropped by the sutler's store just north of Reno Station. Before dismounting, the colonel noticed the unguarded remuda grazing in a pocket ravine on the other side of the river. Inside the store the trader, a longtime frontiersman, assured him that the animals were in no peril; he and the Lakota had always been on good terms.

The words were barely out of the sutler's mouth when one of Col. Carrington's escorts burst into the trading post shouting, "Indians!" The group rushed to the door to watch

A wagon train stops at a trading post in the Sierra Mountains, 1866.
Photo by Lawrence & Houseworth, Library of Congress

Gold miners pose at a camp in California around 1850.
Library of Congress

the trader's animals being stampeded over a rise by a Lakota raiding party.

Carrington's squad galloped back to Reno Station, where the colonel ordered one of his company commanders, Capt. Henry Haymond, to form up a party of ninety men and give chase. Twelve hours later, around one in the morning, the colonel finally spotted the exhausted detail straggling back over a dusty butte.

Capt. Haymond reported that they had ridden fifty miles before losing the Indians; the only animal they could catch was a half-lame Indian pony abandoned during the pursuit.

Eight days later, in the predawn hours of July 16—the hottest day on record across the High Plains in the summer of 1866, with the temperature reaching 111 degrees—Col. Carrington's infantry bade farewell to the small Reno Station and marched northwest. For all its heat, filth, and squalor, the soldiers would soon enough come to recall the station fondly as their last, tenuous link to civilization. The territory beyond, between the little godforsaken post on the north bank of the Powder and the gold camps of Montana, was as mysterious and terrifying as any uncharted sea.

30

The Perfect Fort

Trouble started a mere twelve hours out, along a nearly dry creek bed called Crazy Woman Fork. By that point, nearly half the group's wagons were in need of repair. The wooden wheels had shrunk from the heat, and the metal rims wobbled and fell off. Axles and spokes were also in poor shape. Col. Carrington called a halt, and his wheelwrights fed charcoal bonfires to forge new rims. When the task dragged on longer than expected, the colonel marched on, leaving several companies behind under Capt. Haymond to complete the work.

Not far past Crazy Woman Fork, the trail descended into a long, tight ravine. Before the soldiers reached it, Jim Bridger came racing back. He and Carrington rode ahead to a spot where Bridger pointed at two small pieces of a wooden cracker box, their jagged ends jammed into the dirt at the side of the road.

Scrawled across the wood were terse messages indicating

1151. Sling-Cart for Moving Heavy Cannon.
[FOR DESCRIPTION OF THIS VIEW SEE THE OTHER SIDE OF THIS CARD.]

Stereograph showing an officer leaning against the wheel of a sling cart used to carry heavy artillery.
Library of Congress

that a passing wagon party had beaten off an attack by Indians but lost some of their horses and oxen. Carrington ordered his pickets doubled that night, but there was no sign of Indians. The next day, the battalion reached a plateau bounded on either side by two brooks that Jim Bridger identified as Big Piney Creek and Little Piney Creek. Col. Carrington considered it the perfect site for a fort.

Carrington envisioned three of his companies manning this post while his four remaining companies continued north to establish two more permanent camps. One would straddle the Bighorn River, while the other would rise on the upper Yellowstone River. But the fort here, between the two Piney Creeks, would be the jewel in his crown. He would name it Fort Phil Kearny, in honor of the late Civil War hero.

Jim Bridger appeared to be the only person unhappy with this arrangement. He noted that despite the plateau's proximity to forest, clean water, and rich pasturage, the site was overlooked on three sides by even taller ridges and hills. These heights provided a place where Indians could study the soldiers without consequence. Bridger urged Carrington to keep moving north. The colonel reluctantly complied.

As Carrington led a patrol on a seventy-mile circuit to scout that area, he almost changed his mind and agreed with Bridger. The country north of the Piney Creeks teemed with game; and wild cherries, strawberries, plums, gooseberries, and currants grew in abundance. But the colonel feared that it was too remote from the forested Bighorns to haul wood for construction and winter fires.

Once the patrol returned, Col. Carrington politely but firmly told Bridger that construction would begin the next day atop the plateau. He intended to post daylight pickets on the tallest butte in the area, the nearly mile-high Pilot Knob, a mile due south across Little Piney Creek. Lookouts there would balance any Indian advantage. Bridger had stated his piece and had been overruled. He was not a man to repeat himself.

But now Col. Carrington discovered he had another problem to deal with. He had assumed that once they reached hostile territory, no man would be so foolhardy as to attempt to sneak off by himself. But he had failed to consider the lure of what the Indians called "the yellow metal that makes white men crazy"—gold.

When he returned from his northern scouting mission, he discovered that seven of his enlisted men had deserted for the Montana goldfields. On this occasion, the first of many desertions, the angry colonel sent soldiers up the Bozeman Trail after the runaways. They were stopped seven miles out by a large band of Cheyenne camped near a frontiersman's wagon that had been converted into a mobile trading post. The Indians warned the soldiers they would kill them if they ventured farther north. The soldiers turned back without the deserters but with a message from a Cheyenne head man named Black Horse. He wanted to meet with Carrington, the Little White Chief.

Black Horse and a small group of his subchiefs and warriors arrived at the future site of Fort Phil Kearny under white flag two days later. Carrington's surveying and engineering

Cheyenne head man
Black Horse, wearing
a claw as part of his
headdress, about
1900.
*Photo by Heyn &
Matzen, Library of
Congress*

An 1867 sketch of Fort Phil Kearny by Lt. Jacob Paulus.
Courtesy American Heritage Center, University of Wyoming

skills had already transformed the empty grass plateau into a rectangular seventeen-acre tent city. Black Horse, seemingly impressed, told the colonel through an interpreter that his followers wanted no more war with the whites, but that other members of their tribe, allied with the Lakota and Arapaho, were determined not only to wipe out the interlopers, but to fight any Indian bands who would not join them. Throughout the daylong meeting, Carrington did not need his interpreter to recognize the one name that was mentioned repeatedly—*Makhpiya-luta,* Red Cloud.

Red Cloud was now a Big Belly, Black Horse said, and he explained what that meant. He also stated that Red Cloud had hundreds if not thousands of warriors riding with him. Red Cloud's plan was to cut off the body of the trespassing white snake between here and Reno Station, and eventually all the way south to Fort Laramie. He would then crush the weakened serpent's head beneath his moccasin heel here at Fort Phil Kearny.

The memory of Red Cloud's harsh words at Fort Laramie, of the daggers in the Lakota head man's eyes, and of the big knife in his hand, was fresh in Carrington's mind. The colonel finally realized that Bridger had not been unrealistic with his constant warnings of being watched and studied by Red Cloud from the day they had departed Fort Laramie.

Black Horse told the soldiers that the Bad Faces knew exactly how many soldiers and horses Col. Carrington had posted at Reno Station. They knew the number of men in the smaller party still repairing wagons at Crazy Woman Fork. And Red Cloud and his braves had shadowed Carrington's patrol two days earlier when they had scouted for alternative sites for the post. All this intelligence, Black Horse said, was in service to Red Cloud's desire for a greater understanding of the white soldiers' habits.

Finally, Black Horse mentioned that many of Red Cloud's warriors were at present undergoing a Sun Dance, but there were those who had ridden south toward Reno Station to begin the process of killing the white snake's body. Among the latter was Crazy Horse.

Carrington, Bridger, and the officers present remained stone-faced during the course of the meeting. Despite himself, Carrington found Red Cloud's isolate-and-destroy strategy admirably cool and calculating. While the parley went long into the night, Capt. Haymond and the wagon-repair party arrived from Crazy Woman Fork—one less worry for Carrington. But when the colonel said good-bye to Black Horse and his party at midnight, he was unaware that his Cheyenne visitors were not traveling far. In fact, they halted just a few miles up the Bozeman Trail to camp and trade.

The Cheyenne were in the process of exchanging pelts for various goods, including whiskey, when Red Cloud and a large party of Lakota rode in on them. Red Cloud quizzed Black Horse as to the Little White Chief's intentions. Black Horse told the truth: the soldiers not only would erect a permanent fort between the Little Piney and Big Piney, but also planned to build more posts farther up the trail.

Red Cloud eyed the whiskey jugs and demanded to know why Black Horse and his Cheyenne would bother with these whites. Could the loyalty of the mighty and regal Cheyenne truly be purchased with tobacco, paltry trinkets, and the poisonous *mini wakan*? Where was their pride?

"The white man lies and steals," he said. "My lodges were many, but now they are few. The white man wants all. The white man must fight, and the Indian will die where his fathers died."

Black Horse offered no reply, and in a fit of rage Red Cloud and the Lakota grabbed their bows and quirted the Cheyenne across their faces, shoulders, and backs. This act was unprecedented. Yes, Black Horse and his braves were outnumbered, but they were also important Cheyenne. It was the first time in their lives that these proud men had ever been treated this way. That they did not fight back against this humiliation signaled a new day on the prairie.

This was not only a display of Red Cloud's contempt, but an announcement. There would be no more half measures against the whites, or against anyone who worked with them. As the Lakota rode off, Black Horse and his people immediately packed up and set a course for the mountains. Before leaving, they warned the mobile trading post manager and his partner that they would be wise to do the same, or at least to seek safe harbor in the soldiers' camp between the Piney Creeks.

Meanwhile, several miles to the south, Col. Carrington was discussing with Capt. Haymond a change in orders. The captain had expected to start up the Bozeman Trail the following morning with four companies to scout appropriate sites to build posts. Carrington now had second thoughts about stretching his battalion so thin. Given what he had gleaned from the Cheyenne, further reducing his forces seemed madness, at least until reinforcements arrived.

No, Haymond and his men would remain at Fort Phil Kearny, he decided. The extra hands and strong backs would not only facilitate the transformation of the fort from a tent city into a proper, permanent structure, but also buy time to feel out Red Cloud's movements. And with seven well-armed companies present, the Indians would not dare attempt to strike.

It was as if Red Cloud was reading Carrington's mind. He attacked the next morning.

31

The Rise of Fort Phil Kearny

Captain Haymond awoke at five that morning, when a lookout gave a loud shout. A Lakota raiding party had crept down from the high ground north of the encampment called Lodge Trail Ridge, and one Indian managed to leap onto the troop's lead horse. Before Haymond or any of his men could respond, nearly 175 animals, mostly mules, were being stampeded back over the ridge. The easterners were now to learn their first lesson in Indian fighting: never give chase to a raiding party without a close-knit and overwhelming force.

Capt. Haymond and an enlisted man immediately took off on their horses, but the rest of the troop had difficulty rounding up and saddling their skittish mounts. Haymond was nearly out of sight by the time the troop, in scattered groups of three and four, followed the dust cloud of stolen animals. When the Indians saw the haphazard pursuit, braves began dropping back and circling around in ambush. One trooper took an arrow to his chest; another was blasted out of his saddle by a musket ball. Reinforcements eventually caught up to Haymond's party and engaged in a running fight stretching along a fifteen-mile length of the trail. They were too late for the two dead and three seriously wounded men in Haymond's command. Nor did the Americans manage to retrieve their mules and horses, which had vanished onto the prairie.

On the slow, bitter ride back to the fort, the troop found the mobile post trader and his partner splayed across the dusty saw grass. They had been scalped and mutilated. A few yards away, four teamsters were discovered similarly violated.

The soldiers had of course heard stories of Indian atrocities, but this was their first personal encounter. One private noted in his journal that "it gave us all a most convincing lesson on what our fate would be should we fall into [their] hands."

Over the next week, Fort Phil Kearny began to rise. Under Col. Carrington, the soldiers were temporarily transformed from a fighting troop into loggers, blacksmiths, carpenters, teamsters, hay mowers, painters, and shingle makers. The colonel established a tree-cutting camp, what he called a pinery, in the mountain forest to provide wood.

The walls of the fort consisted of more than 4,000 logs, with firing loopholes bored through every fourth one. This stockade would soon contain barracks, officers' quarters, warehouses, administration buildings, a sutler's store, an infirmary, and an underground magazine to store ammunition. These buildings would surround a parade ground complete with a bandstand. Such was Carrington's attention to detail that he issued orders that no one was to walk on the grass.

Red Cloud was enraged from the first *thwunck* of ax blades gouging the trunks of the ninety-foot pines on what the Americans had dubbed Piney Island. His scouts kept up a constant surveillance of the woodchoppers, though this was hardly necessary. The whine of the sawmill and the crash of falling timber could be heard for miles—a reminder of the defilement of *Wakan Tanka.*

In the last week of June, Col. Carrington sent a company of infantry back to Reno Station for sacks of foodstuffs he had not been able to haul on the initial trip north. As a precaution, Jim Bridger was ordered to accompany them. Sixteen hours later, the colonel's orderly and a courier, covered with dust, awakened him at one o'clock in the morning. Not only had his freight train been ambushed, but three other emigrant trains in the vicinity were also under attack. Carrington was dumbfounded. Red Cloud had orchestrated four simultaneous engagements. It was unheard of. The colonel had no idea that farther south, near Crazy Woman Fork, an even larger party of Lakota had pinned down a relief column that included the battalion's five replacement officers.

32

Roughing It

The simultaneous Indian attacks had only managed to take the lives of three of Col. Carrington's soldiers, including a lieutenant traveling north as part of a group of replacement officers. But they had convinced Col. Carrington that Red Cloud, unlike any of the Plains war chiefs, not only was qualified to plan and carry out multiple skirmishes, but also encouraged his raiding parties to employ various tactics, from surprise ambushes to head-on engagements. This was a new strategy for the Sioux.

Carrington finally received a dispatch from Gen. Philip Cooke stating that he could expect no more reinforcements until sometime in the fall. At the same time, the War Department remained anxious over the lack of forts farther up the Bozeman Trail. Carrington was in a bind. He had already sent another infantry company south to support the garrison at Reno Station. The thought of giving up two more of his remaining six companies to erect a third outpost seemed foolish.

Carrington's fear led him to make a risky decision: he bypassed the chain of command and wrote directly to the adjutant general in Washington, outlining his predicament and requesting assistance. Perhaps to soften this breach of military protocol, he also wrote a long report to Gen. Cooke, to be carried by the same mail courier. In it he took what he hoped was a more peacemaking tone.

"Character of Indian affairs hostile," he began. "The treaty does not yet benefit this route." He then once again compiled the long list of complaints he had been filing since his arrival at Fort Laramie. How could he be expected to build forts and fight Indians and safeguard more than 500 miles of the Bozeman Trail with so few resources?

His horses, accustomed to eating oats, were weak from consuming nothing but hay. His weapons were outdated. His ammunition was rationed. His best officers were being recalled. His infantrymen could barely ride. And the emigrant wagon trains were led by civilians who refused to pay attention to his orders. Finally, he added, he was acting not only as his own engineer and construction-gang boss but as a military strategist and tactician against an exceedingly shrewd enemy who picked off his men and his stock in small daily engagements yet refused to come out and fight a proper battle. "I must do all this, however arduous," he concluded, "and say I have not the men."

This was all true. The War Department had never

developed any formal strategy for dealing with guerrilla attacks. Yet however much Col. Carrington believed he was merely stating the obvious, to the battle-tested generals who read his report he seemed to be whining and unprofessional. Rather than attempt to learn as much about their enemy as possible, Carrington's superiors—like the long, sad succession of Indian-fighting soldiers before them—just wanted Red Cloud eliminated. It would be another ten weeks before Capt. Fetterman was sent west to straighten out this mess, but by then official ignorance had already doomed Col. Carrington's command.

33

A Flood of Attacks

As the troops in the Powder River Country awaited the arrival of the reinforcements accompanying Capt. Fetterman, the disturbing dispatches from the frontier that were reaching the War Department in Washington turned from a trickle into a flood. The reports, read today, are all the more disheartening for their matter-of-fact depictions of death and destruction. The journal of one of Col. Carrington's officers, Capt. Tenedor Ten Eyck, is representative of this. A few samples:

> **July 29**: A "citizen train" was attacked by Indians near the South Fork of the Cheyenne, and eight men were killed and two injured. One of the injured men later died from his wounds.

> **August 6**: A train lost two civilians killed by Indians along the 236-mile trail between Forts Laramie and

Phil Kearny. Later that night, another train traveling the same route lost fifteen killed and five wounded.

August 7: Indians made their first coordinated attack on the wood train on the road from Piney Island, killing one teamster.

August 12: Indians raided a civilian train near the Powder, running off a large stock of cattle and horses.

August 13: Indians attacked the Piney Island wood train again; no casualties were sustained.

August 14: Indians killed two civilians less than a mile from Reno Station.

August 17: An Indian raiding party entered Reno Station's corral and stole seventeen mules and seven of the garrison's twenty-two horses.

September 8: Under cover of lashing rain, Indians stampeded twenty horses and mules that belonged to a civilian contractor who was delivering barrels of ham, bacon, hardtack, soap, flour, sugar, and coffee to Fort Phil Kearny.

September 10: Indians returned and made off with another forty-two mules. While the raiders led an army patrol on a futile chase, another band took advantage of the post's weakened defenses to fall on the battalion's herd a mile from the stockade and sweep away thirty-three horses and seventy-eight more mules.

September 12: An Indian war party ambushed a hay-mowing detail, killing three and wounding six.

September 13: A combined Lakota-Arapaho raiding party, several hundred braves in total, stampeded a buffalo drove into the post's cattle herd grazing near Peno Creek. Two pickets were wounded; 209 head of cattle were lost in the buffalo run.

September 14: Two privates were killed by Indians, one while attempting to desert and the other after riding too far ahead of a hay train. Wolves made off with both bodies. Two hay-mowing machines were destroyed, and a large quantity of baled hay was burned.

September 22: The scalped, stripped, and mutilated bodies of three civilian freighters returning from Montana were discovered eleven miles from the post.

These raids and attacks went on through October and November, until it was evident even to the army leadership that in Red Cloud the Indians had finally found a war chief who could coordinate and sustain an effective military campaign.

The Bozeman Trail was extraordinarily vulnerable. Every few miles offered an ideal ridgeline, draw, or mesa from which a small, swift war party could harass a clumsy wagon train with deadly accuracy. The Indians knew the land so well that when army patrols were assembled to chase them, they would vanish into countless ravines and breaks. And when parties of mounted Bluecoats did cut off a large body of hostiles, the engagement left their supply wagons vulnerable to secondary attacks, a tactic that Red Cloud perfected.

As tales of the lawless, bloody Bozeman Trail attacks trickled back east, newspapers from St. Louis to New York eagerly published the stories. Still the settlers and miners came—individuals, families, entire clans—drawn by the vast swaths of free land, by the mountains filled with minerals, by the same spirit of freedom that had drawn their ancestors from Europe to the shores of the New World. August 1866 was the high point of emigration on the Oregon Trail, with at least one wagon train arriving per day at Col. Carrington's Fort Phil Kearny. Many emigrants were also gratified to find women and children living at the post. Families meant civilization, if only its razor-thin edge.

But nothing could prepare the easterners for the difficulties of life at the fort. Unlike older and more established posts such as Fort Laramie—which boasted a circulating library, a regular amateur theater, and even an occasional fancy ball—Fort Phil Kearny was "roughing it" in the true sense of the phrase.

Under the broiling summer sun, the stench of human and animal sweat and waste hung over the post like an illness. And with the exception of noncommissioned officers, who were granted their own small rooms within the barracks, all enlisted men lived in an open bay heated in the winter by cast-iron stoves. The fort's buildings were stifling in summer and "breezy in winter." As the logs and boards shrank, the

Logging on the frontier required sturdy horses and men, all of which had to be guarded. These are civilian loggers.
Photo by Darius Kinsey, 1905, Library of Congress

gaps were stuffed with sod, which was blown away by a good wind; and rain and snow—either falling through the cracks or dragged in on boots—turned the dirt floors to carpets of mud.

While Fort Phil Kearny may have been gaining families, it was fast losing men. In the first week of August, Col. Carrington finally gave in to the War Department and sent two companies north to scout positions for a fort on the Bighorn. It would be named in honor of the Mexican War hero Gen. C. F. Smith. Bridger went along to guide the expedition, but was instructed to return as soon as a suitable site was found.

Not long after his two companies marched north—leading a long line of civilian trains that had been awaiting an escort into Montana—Col. Carrington was forced to supply a personal bodyguard of twenty-seven of his best men to a visiting brigadier general on a tour of the Bozeman Trail. The general never returned the men.

By early autumn, Fort Phil Kearny was stretched to its limit. The wood trains to and from Piney Island required constant security details, and continuous daylight lookouts were stationed on top of the Sullivant Hills and Pilot Knob, the two highest points surrounding the fort. In addition, there were regular distress calls from emigrant trains under attack. Col. Carrington was like a chess player forced to begin his match with only eight pieces. His roster at the fort was down to just under 350 officers and men—a fact he was certain Red Cloud knew as well as he.

Meanwhile, during a layover at Fort Laramie, Gen. Sherman met with several of the Sioux subchiefs who had signed

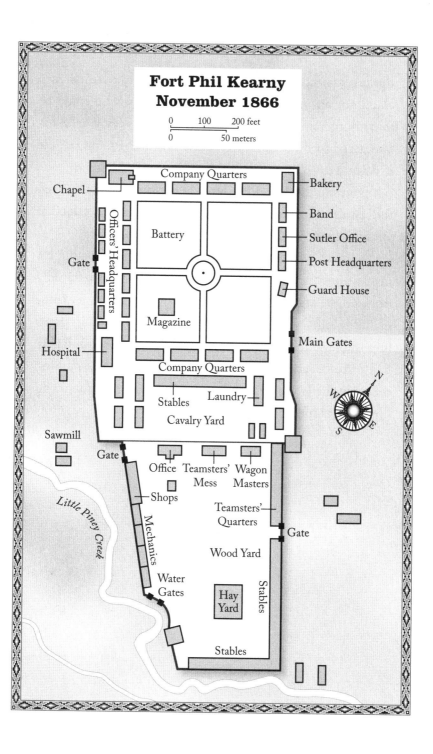

Fort Phil Kearny
November 1866

0   100   200 feet

0   50 meters

Chapel

Company Quarters

Bakery

Officers' Headquarters

Band

Battery

Sutler Office

Post Headquarters

Gate

Guard House

Magazine

Hospital

Main Gates

Company Quarters

Stables

Laundry

Cavalry Yard

Sawmill

Gate

Office

Teamsters' Mess

Wagon Masters

Shops

Little Piney Creek

Teamsters' Quarters

Gate

Mechanics

Wood Yard

Stables

Water Gates

Hay Yard

Stables

N
W   E
S

the previous spring's treaty. When they admitted that they could not always restrain their young braves, who could be rash, from joining Red Cloud's raiding parties, Sherman's famous temper flared, his red whiskers seeming to bristle. He had heard too much of this excuse. Turning to his interpreters but pointing dramatically toward the Indians, he said, "Tell the rascals so are mine; and if another white man is scalped in all this region, it will be impossible to hold mine in."

Sherman penned a letter to Col. Carrington making his instructions clear. "We must try and distinguish friendly from hostile and kill the latter, but if you or any other commanding officer strike a blow I will approve, for it seems impossible to tell the true from the false." Carrington barely had to read between the lines. The second-highest-ranking officer in the U.S. Army had just declared open season on all High Plains Indians, friend or foe.

34

Scalped Alive

A few days after Sherman's declaration, three Piney Island woodcutters were ambushed in a thick section of forest. Two of these enlisted men escaped to the island's blockhouse with minor wounds. They told of watching their fallen comrade, Private Patrick Smith, shot through with arrows and scalped. Incredibly, Smith had not been killed, and he crawled half a mile back to the American lines. He was rushed by ambulance to the fort, where he died.

That night at mess, graphic stories were told and retold of Smith's death. Scalped alive. Left for dead with the skin hanging in strips from his forehead. Arrows deliberately aimed to wound rather than to kill. It was unusually bad timing when nine Cheyenne, professing friendship, rode up to the fort near twilight and Col. Carrington granted them permission to camp at Little Piney Creek. Someone started a rumor that they were the same Indians who had killed Pat Smith.

Capt. Tenedor Ten Eyck.
Courtesy American Heritage Center, University of Wyoming

It spread rapidly through the barracks, with the troopers expressing the same conviction as Sherman: it is impossible to tell the true from the false.

Around midnight, some ninety men crept from their bunks and scaled the post's walls. But the chaplain woke Col. Carrington. Carrington roused Capt. Ten Eyck, who in turn gathered an armed guard. They arrived just in time to prevent the massacre. The mob tried to scatter, but two shots from Carrington's Colt froze them.

The colonel and Capt. Ten Eyck recognized among the crowd some of their best fighting men. They took a moment to confer and concluded that they could not afford to discipline the men. Taking the Indians' side might alienate the troops. The post's tiny guardhouse already held twenty-four prisoners, most of them caught deserting. The battalion was in fact averaging a desertion every other day, and harsh discipline meted out here would only spur more "gold runners." Carrington ordered the Cheyenne away, gathered the angry soldiers, and settled for a "brief tongue lashing" before marching them back to their quarters.

The colonel was still contemplating this incident when Jim Bridger returned from the north country where soldiers were constructing Fort C. F. Smith. The Crows had told Bridger that Red Cloud was camped along the headwaters of the Tongue River, not seventy miles away, where there were also about 500 lodges of Lakota, Arapaho, and a few Gros Ventres. This meant anywhere from 500 to 1,000 warriors, including the soldier societies. Bridger said that hostile Northern Cheyenne were also in the vicinity, camped along

Rosebud Creek, and that the Crows had told him it took half a day to ride through the villages.

All told, it was the largest combined Indian force Bridger had ever heard of, and there was talk of destroying the white soldiers' two forts. For once Bridger looked concerned. He paced along the compound's battlements, "constantly scanning the opposite hills that commanded a good view of the fort as if he suspected Indians of having scouts behind every sage clump or fallen cottonwood."

35

Fire in the Belly

Moments past daybreak on Monday, September 17, Red Cloud struck again.

A large war party of Lakota and Arapaho rode down into the little valley east of Fort Phil Kearny at the juncture of Big Piney and Little Piney Creeks. They took what was left of the American's dwindled cattle herd—only 50 cows remained out of the 700 that had begun the trip through Nebraska.

The pickets, no strangers by now to surprise attacks, were confused to find the Indians firing revolvers. The raiders stampeded the animals, but the post was prepared. Capt. Frederick Brown immediately mounted a detail. The Indians had come to recognize Brown from his hair—a small rim of hair around a bald spot—and had given him the nickname Bald Head Eagle. Fortunately, Brown thrived on his assignment—so much so that, with Col. Carrington's unspoken approval, he was stalling transfer orders to Fort Laramie that he had received a week earlier.

As Brown's detail charged from the corral, Carrington ordered his twelve-pound field howitzer fired. The shells burst among the Indians, driving them back into the hills and scattering the cattle. Within minutes, Brown and his men had recaptured the herd, and they were driving the cattle back toward the fort when they crossed paths with an army supply train coming up the Bozeman Trail. It had just delivered ammunition to Reno Station and was carrying another 60,000 rounds for Fort Phil Kearny. Among the train's passengers were two civilian surgeons as well as a replacement officer, the Civil War veteran 2nd Lt. George Washington Grummond. Grummond was traveling with his pregnant wife, Frances.

Grummond was an odd case. On the one hand, he was the kind of experienced fighter you wanted by your side in Indian country. On the other, he was frightening. A stormy-tempered alcoholic, he had risen from sergeant to lieutenant during the war for his aggressive, if reckless, tactics.

Frances Grummond would later write about their approach to the fort: "My whole being seemed to be absorbed in the one desire, an agonized but un-uttered cry, 'Let me get within the gate!'. . . That strange feeling of apprehension never left me." Mrs. Grummond spent a restless first night at Fort Phil Kearny, finally falling asleep sometime after midnight. When she and her husband awoke the next morning, their tent was buried beneath a foot of snow.

In October 1866, the rift between the various bands of Lakota widened. Indian agents were once again putting out feelers about treaties, and with winter approaching and more gifts in mind, some Oglalas were inclined to listen. One of them was Old Man Afraid of His Horses.

Although technically still a Big Belly, Old Man Afraid of His Horses had reverted to subtle calls for diplomacy. As a result, the most hostile tribal factions started to gravitate toward Red Cloud, now recognized as the supreme Lakota war chief, the *blotahunka ataya*.

The banks of the prairie creeks were crusting over with ice, and Red Cloud was now forty-five. In earlier days he would have been free to rest on his reputation as a warrior who had proved himself again and again and enjoy life—to grow fat hunting deer, buffalo, and antelope; to sire more children; to instruct his children and their children in the old ways.

Instead, when the Little White Chief—Col. Carrington— had sent his Bluecoats north to the Bighorn to build a second fort, it was Red Cloud who sponsored a formal war-pipe council among the Lakota and Northern Cheyenne. He proposed a major offensive against the original fort between the Piney Creeks once the snows completely cut off communications between the whites. This was a completely new strategy for the Indians, who rarely fought during the winter months.

Red Cloud had attracted a large contingent of Miniconjou, Sans Arcs, and Brule fighters to his cause, and he had personally recruited warriors from formerly neutral Arapaho bands. Further, in late August he swept aside a century of blood hatred to lead a group to meet with the Crows. At the main Crow village, he asked his old enemies to join the war against the whites. As part of the bargain, he offered to return to the tribe a portion of the old hunting grounds east of the mountains that the Sioux had previously taken.

The bid was unsuccessful. Although several Crow braves were eager to don war paint against the whites, their head men remained noncommittal, promising only to reciprocate with a visit to the Bad Face camp. But the fact that Red Cloud dared to break long-standing tradition, and that some Crows had considered fighting alongside the Lakota, was evidence of the desperate High Plains Indians' extraordinary crisis.

Red Cloud had also begun to draw into his inner circle the maturing Crazy Horse, the leader of a cohort of young fighters who increasingly looked to the *blotahunka ataya* for guidance and direction. The gruff, physically imposing Big Belly and the slim warrior nineteen years his junior made an unlikely pair.

There was no question that Crazy Horse and his Strong Hearts had been responsible for most of the destruction along the lower Bozeman Trail through the summer. The Strong Hearts had marauded as far south and east as Fort Laramie, and Crazy Horse had led the raiding party that sneaked into the Reno Station corral to run off the horses and mules one week before he ambushed the white soldiers at Crazy Woman Fork.

As the weather had turned and the white settler trains thinned, the Strong Hearts had moved north to harass the woodcutting and hay-mowing groups from Fort Phil Kearny. When Crazy Horse intermittently returned from these raids, there was always a seat awaiting him at Red Cloud's council

A supply train caught in a snowstorm on the plains.
Library of Congress

fire. Crazy Horse had never shown interest in mundane tribal politics—the elections of subchiefs, the planning of hunts, the debates over future campsites—but now that the talk centered on killing whites, he was often present, though he hardly ever spoke.

As the last civilian trains of the season made haste for Montana before winter snows blocked the north country's valleys and passes, two commissary caravans pulled into Fort Phil Kearny from Nebraska. Together they had hauled nearly 180,000 pounds of corn and more than 20,000 pounds of oats, enough grain to carry the post's weakened mounts through midwinter. When Col. Carrington and Capt. Brown inspected their remuda, they determined that only forty horses were strong enough for the pursuit of the Indians.

The supply trains also brought a cache of much-needed medical supplies; but, as with the horse feed, Carrington realized that these would not last until spring.

Good news arrived late that October with the return of the bodyguard Col. Carrington had lent to the visiting brigadier general. The lead officer reported that the new northern post, situated so close to friendly Crow country, had yet to be attacked.

A courier delivered a disturbing letter from Gen. Cooke. In it the general seemed to assume that a company of men had recently arrived to reinforce Fort Phil Kearny—although in fact none had. Cooke "strongly recommended" that, since Carrington now possessed an abundance of mounts, he send his surplus horses to Fort Laramie to aid in its defense. A company of cavalry? Surplus horses? Was Cooke out of his mind?

The situation was not improved when, soon after Gen. Cooke's letter arrived, another courier rode into Fort Phil Kearny, with orders from Gen. Sherman officially abolishing the title of that area, "Mountain District." This was mostly a bureaucratic formality; Col. Carrington's orders to keep the Powder River Country safe for travelers remained in place. In fact, the order's real impact was a blessing, because the colonel found himself relieved of dealing with stacks and stacks of extra paperwork.

The name change, however, did highlight one crucial difference between Col. Carrington and Red Cloud. Unlike Carrington, Red Cloud both made the rules and carried out battle plans. In Carrington's case, generals hundreds if not thousands of miles from Fort Phil Kearny concocted the strategy and tactics and expected their agent on the scene to carry them out. Red Cloud was on the scene, a strategic and tactical genius running circles around the Little White Chief. Although he never mentioned it or wrote of it, Col. Carrington was probably aware of this.

To show that the dissolution of the Mountain District designation was by no means a slight on his men's (and his) performance, and to celebrate the return of the visiting general's escort detail, the colonel declared the last day of October a holiday.

A day earlier, the troopers had been issued new uniforms to replace the patched, mended rags some had been wearing since the Civil War. The morning of the celebration, every man, weapon, and mount was lined up for review on the small plain between the stockade and Big Piney Creek.

The band played, cannons were fired, and a moment of silence was observed for those who had lost their lives. When a great luncheon on the parade ground was complete, the chaplain stepped forward to offer a prayer and Col. Carrington signaled to his flag bearers.

For the past week, a pair of enlisted men had been putting the finishing touches on the garrison's crowning achievement: a 124-foot flagpole. Now the two enlisted men approached the pole. The regimental band played "Hail Columbia" as they unfurled an enormous American flag, twenty by thirty-six feet, and hoisted the Stars and Stripes, to a loud cheer.

It was the first U.S. garrison flag to fly between the North Platte and the Yellowstone, and the vibrant red, white, and blue waving high above the prairie would serve as a beacon to travelers coming up the Bozeman Trail. After the official ceremonies, for the first time since their arrival at Fort Phil Kearny 106 days earlier, the 360 officers and enlisted men were given permission to loaf the rest of the afternoon.

Two hours later, they were recalled to their posts when Indians flashing mirror signals appeared on Lodge Trail Ridge. Among the hostiles were Red Cloud and Crazy Horse.

PART FIVE

The Massacre

When a man moves from nature, his heart becomes
hard. —*Lakota proverb*

36

Fetterman

Crazy Horse was already in the surrounding hills looking for raiding opportunities when the soldiers ran up their flag and fired their big guns. He sent messengers with word of this strange behavior, and Red Cloud joined the large, curious group riding south to see what the commotion was about. It was pure chance that so many Indians arrived on the bluffs overlooking Fort Phil Kearny hours before the last civilian train of the season pulled into the post.

Red Cloud had not sent any war parties south to Reno Station for weeks, assuming the whites were done traveling for the season. For precisely this reason, the train had rolled up the Bozeman Trail unscathed, and its security measures were lax. That night, after the wagon master conferred with Colonel Carrington, the settlers dutifully circled their prairie schooners on the little plain a hundred yards from the fort—where, earlier in the day, the garrison had been inspected—securing them wheel to wheel with ropes and enclosing the stock within.

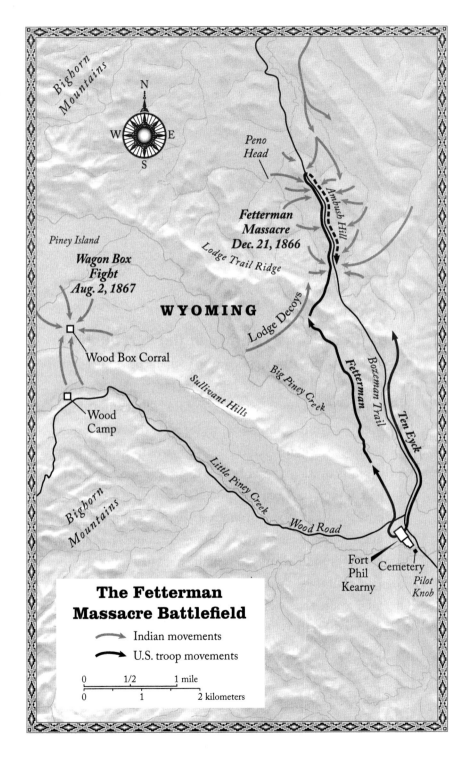

Bighorn Mountains

N
W E
S

Peno Head

Fetterman Massacre
Dec. 21, 1866

Ambush Hill

Piney Island

Wagon Box Fight
Aug. 2, 1867

Lodge Trail Ridge

WYOMING

Wood Box Corral

Lodge Decoys

Big Piney Creek

Sullivant Hills

Wood Camp

Bozeman Trail

Fetterman

Ten Eyck

Little Piney Creek

Bighorn Mountains

Wood Road

Fort Phil Kearny   Cemetery

Pilot Knob

The Fetterman Massacre Battlefield

⟶ Indian movements

⟶ U.S. troop movements

0   1/2   1 mile
0   1   2 kilometers

But the travelers' guard was down. A few of them lit campfires and sat around the flames playing cards as a party of Strong Hearts crept near. The Indians let loose a volley of arrows. One man was killed instantly; two more were wounded. The Lakota vanished by the time the panicked emigrants began firing blindly into the darkness.

It was good to kill the white trespassers, but the attack so close to the fort also served another purpose. Afterward, the Indians lit their own bonfires on the hills overlooking the post and danced furiously, boldly flitting into and out of shadows cast by the flames. It was a reminder to the soldiers of whose territory they dared occupy.

It was also a mistake. The Bluecoats hauled out their howitzers and bombarded the dancers with grapeshot. Several Indians were killed or wounded.

After the shelling, angry warriors argued that now was the time to strike the Americans in force, to wipe out the post and all within it. The autumn buffalo hunt was completed. The Upper Powder tribes were strong and united. What was Red Cloud waiting for? The *blotahunka ataya* asked for patience. Not yet, he said. But soon enough. There were, his scouts had informed him, more white soldiers on the way.

On the morning of November 3, 1866, Capt. William Judd Fetterman crested Pilot Knob within sight of Fort Phil Kearny. It was two days after the attack on the year's last civilian wagon train bound for Montana.

Despite his unfamiliarity with the frontier, Fetterman surely admired what he saw. Inside the stout pine walls,

Capt. William Judd Fetterman's life dream was to have a military career. *Courtesy American Heritage Center, University of Wyoming*

Lt. George Grummond consistently underestimated the skill and numbers of his Indian opponents. *Courtesy Library of Congress*

dozens of buildings had been completed or were nearing completion, and from the top of Pilot Knob, the post gave the impression of a good place to conduct his hunt for Red Cloud.

Once through the main gate, Fetterman and the sixty-three horsemen under his command were greeted with sighs of relief. The incessant Indian attacks over the previous months had left the post's inhabitants on edge, and the mounted reinforcements led by one of the regiment's most decorated officers were a welcome sight. Before Fetterman even dismounted, he was hailed warmly by his Civil War comrades Capt. Brown and Lt. William Bisbee, his old quartermaster and adjutant from the Atlanta campaign.

On the journey from Omaha, he had also become close to one of his junior officers, Capt. James Powell. Soon the feisty Lt. George Grummond fell into his orbit also. Together with scores of enlisted men who had followed him through some of the war's bloodiest battles they would form a clique. These men felt they could clear the Indians from the territory in a snap if only Col. Carrington would unleash them.

It did not take Capt. Fetterman long to identify the obstacles. Like all the officers deployed to the Powder River Country, Capt. Brown and Lt. Bisbee could recite the disturbing statistics from memory. Since the army's arrival in July, there had been fifty-one attacks on the post and its surroundings. One hundred fifty-four soldiers and civilians had been killed, and at least three times that number had been wounded.

Not a single wagon train had reached Montana without

violent loss of life. More than 800 head of army livestock had been stolen, in addition to an untold number of emigrants' horses, mules, cattle, and oxen. And though it was not yet winter, the government had already ordered the Bozeman Trail closed until the following summer. It was too unsafe for civilian traffic.

In that time, Col. Carrington had not undertaken one offensive operation against the hostiles. This inaction was embarrassing to the junior officers at Fort Phil Kearny; worse, for the nineteenth-century U.S. Army, it reflected dishonorably on the post and the garrison.

Accompanying Capt. Fetterman and Capt. Powell had been two additional officers—the infantry company commander Maj. Henry Almstedt and a young cavalry lieutenant named Horatio Bingham. Almstedt had come west carrying a satchel of greenbacks, the battalion's payroll, and James Wheatley's little restaurant just outside the fort saw an immediate increase in customers.

The influx of new men raised the strength of the garrison to some 400 effective troops; but despite the almost 200 additional armed civilian teamsters, hay mowers, and pinery workers, this was a modest number of able bodies, and it surely struck Capt. Fetterman as too few to police the vast territory he had just crossed.

Meanwhile, the Crows had again offered the Americans their services—250 mounted warriors to join the war against their old enemies the Lakota. These braves knew the countryside intimately; it had once been theirs. They were also wise to the ways of Red Cloud.

Colonel Carrington declined. It was not merely a question of expense, although the Crow head men would undoubtedly want a hefty fee for their services. Carrington had received no word from Gen. Cooke in Omaha about his request for the use of the company of exceptional Winnebago Indian scouts from Iowa but he still hoped. He reasoned that fifty Winnebagos with rifles trumped five times as many Crows with bows and arrows.

Capt. Fetterman outranked Capt. Ten Eyck by several months' service, so he immediately replaced him as Carrington's principal tactical officer. As part of this role, Fetterman conducted his own troop inspection shortly after his arrival. He was appalled at the condition of the garrison, particularly the inadequate weaponry.

Before his departure from Omaha, Fetterman had been informed that the Frontier Army was planning yet another reorganization, scheduled for January 1, 1867. Gen. Cooke hinted strongly that Capt. Fetterman would replace Col. Carrington as the battalion's commanding officer. Fetterman was a hungry soldier, eager for advancement, and not a man to allow his cordial prewar relationship with his superior, Carrington, to stand in the way of his own ambition. To that end, he moved quickly to make his presence known, both to Red Cloud and to the War Department. He got his chance on his third day at the fort.

That evening, Fetterman approached Carrington after dinner with a plan to turn the Indians' own tactics against them. He proposed to hobble a string of mules to serve as decoys near a thicket of cottonwoods along Big Piney Creek about a mile from the post. He and a company of infantry would conceal themselves in the nearby trees and fall on any Indians who took the bait.

He said he had talked over the idea with Capt. Brown and Lt. Grummond, who wanted to join the ambush. Carrington granted him permission. Fetterman, Brown, Grummond, Lt. Bisbee, and about fifty enlisted men settled into the cottonwood stand shortly after dusk. Their rifles were primed and cocked, but the only movements they saw all night were meteors streaking across the big Wyoming sky.

Near dawn, as they were getting ready to return to the post, they heard shots from the opposite side of the stockade. A mile away from their position, Indian raiders—aware of the ruse from the outset—had stampeded a small herd of cattle belonging to the civilian innkeepers.

Despite the failed trap, it is apparent in hindsight that Fetterman's arrival had the War Department's intended effect on Col. Carrington. Two days later, in a dispatch to Gen. Cooke, Carrington described Red Cloud's increasing strength and concluded, "I . . . hope yet to be able to strike a blow."

He had never expressed such a desire before. Meanwhile, as Capt. Fetterman acclimated to life at the fort, his disdain for Col. Carrington's passivity intensified into nearly open contempt, and he wrote to an old friend, "We are afflicted with an incompetent commanding officer."

Yet despite his and the others' "disgust" with the colonel, the era's code of conduct, both military and social, prevented open insubordination. One officer noted that "the feeling was not harmonious" between Capt. Carrington and the young soldiers, "but there was no open rupture." At least for the moment.

Meanwhile, Red Cloud intensified his harassment of the post itself, turning loose Crazy Horse and the Strong Hearts to darken the snow-covered ground with American blood. A beef contractor driving a herd up the Bozeman Trail was attacked, and the raids on the wood trains to and from Piney Island escalated.

Through their keen observation, his young warriors recognized that the best time to strike at the whites was either early in the morning, when their minds were still hazy with sleep, or late in the afternoon, when they were exhausted from a day of chopping wood or ice. Crazy Horse followed through with a series of ambushes and hit-and-run attacks, which left the fort's surgeons perilously low on medical supplies.

Red Cloud was satisfied with the physical damage he was inflicting, though he was probably not aware of the psychological toll his tactics were taking on the isolated garrison. With every dead or wounded trooper, with every stolen horse or mule, with every whistle of an arrow and crack of a Hawken, the tension at the fort heightened. Bickering among the soldiers intensified. The troop at Fort Phil Kearny was disintegrating under the weight of petty feuds and traded insults. The underlying problem, Capt. Fetterman and his friends were certain, stemmed from Col. Carrington's refusal to actually engage with the Indians.

Indian attacks continued as the snow piled high; and with no more emigrant trains as diversion, the arrival of couriers with news of the outside world grew rare, the remote stillness of Fort Phil Kearny—interrupted only by shrieking war cries—began to fray men's nerves.

The soldiers could not know that after five months of raids and ambushes, the Indians were nearly as weary of Red Cloud's slow, fitful campaign. By this time of year, all the tribes should have been ensconced in comfortable winter camps—the Sioux and Cheyenne in sheltered wooded hollows near the Black Hills, the Arapaho off toward the Rockies.

There men would sleep late after trading stories well into the night around warming fires, and pass the dreary afternoons fashioning new bows and arrows surrounded by pipe smoke. Instead, the warriors now spent their days greasing their limbs against the bitter cold. They prepared for creeping around the open prairie or forested hills wrapped in stinking wolf skins and inverted buffalo robes, their high-topped buffalo-fur moccasins soaked through and freezing—all in the hope of running across a straggling Bluecoat and putting an arrow through his throat.

Ironically, it was now the once quiet Crazy Horse whose voice was loudest at the council fires. He urged the war chiefs to attack in force, to strike a single, final blow against the soldiers. But Red Cloud was hesitant. He had planned to starve and weaken the Americans. But he also recognized that it might not be wise to ignore the words of his best fighter. He had always respected Crazy Horse's tactics; perhaps it was time to heed his young lieutenant's strategy as well. Perhaps it was time to test the Americans where they lived.

Dress Rehearsal

On the morning of December 6, Red Cloud mounted his finest war pony and left his camp at the head of several hundred angry warriors. The temperature was below freezing, creeks flowed beneath thick ice, and wispy gray clouds moved down from the Bighorns on a biting wind that scoured the prairie.

When the Indians reached the small, flat valley on the far side of Lodge Trail Ridge from Fort Phil Kearny, about a hundred braves broke west, circled behind the edge of the ridge, and descended into the timber around Piney Island. With ferocious screams and shrieking whistles, they immediately fell on a wood train and its escort returning from the pinery. A messenger made the dangerous four-mile ride back to the post to alert Col. Carrington, who ordered every serviceable horse saddled. If Gen. Cooke wanted offensive action, Carrington would give it to him.

Col. Carrington directed Capt. Fetterman and Lt. Bingham to lead just over fifty men due west up the wood road to relieve the train and drive the attackers back across the creek. In the meantime he and Lt. Grummond, at the head of another squad of twenty-four horsemen, would race north up Lodge Trail Ridge to intercept the retreating Indians, trapping them in the valley. As Carrington galloped up the south bank of Big Piney Creek, he saw Indians above him lining the crest of Lodge Trail Ridge to his right. He signaled his squad to cross the creek, but his own mount slipped and floundered on the ice sheet and threw him from the saddle. He remounted and made the crossing, and he and Lt. Grummond led the troopers up the steep slope.

They were greeted at the crest by four Indians, their ponies straddling the wagon ruts of the Bozeman Trail several hundred yards away. More were trying to conceal themselves in thick stands of chokecherry and scrub oak, but Col. Carrington had reached the ridgeline sooner than they expected and he spotted them, counting at least thirty-two.

Instead of attacking, Carrington concentrated on the wood road below him to his left, where at this moment he saw another fifty or so hostiles galloping out of the timber. Fetterman's and Bingham's detail was in hot pursuit. The colonel drove off the four taunting braves with a volley and pointed downslope. After many frustrating months, it was time to spring his own trap.

Carrington cautioned his inexperienced riders against scattering, and ordered them to pick their way slowly down the face of the ridge that descended into the Peno Creek valley. But Lt. Grummond ignored him and spurred his mount to a gallop. Events worsened from there.

Lt. Grummond put so much distance between himself and Col. Carrington's squad that the fuming Carrington sent his best rider to overtake him with orders to either halt "or return to the post." The messenger could not catch Grummond, who disappeared into the valley's tangle of ravines and draws. The colonel's anger increased when he reached the bottom of the incline and came across fifteen dismounted cavalrymen from Bingham's command, looking thoroughly confounded. He ordered them folded into his squad and took off at a trot without bothering to look back to see if they had actually saddled up.

They had not. A quarter mile later he reached a small hill, the only way around it a thin trail. He expected to find the lieutenants Grummond and Bingham somewhere on the other side. Instead, when he rounded the rise, his path was blocked by several dozen Indians on horseback.

He turned to give skirmish orders. Only six of his inexperienced riders were still with him. One of them was Lt. Bingham's bugler, a German immigrant named Adolph Metzger. Carrington sputtered to the little bugler, "Where is Lt. Bingham?" Metzger, whose command of English was limited, pointed past the Indians. Carrington immediately surmised that the hostiles had doubled back, hidden in the folds of the hill, and allowed Fetterman's and Bingham's larger party to ride on in order to confront him. The trap had been sprung.

The Indians whooped and charged, and at the same

moment a few straggling soldiers caught up to Carrington. One trooper's mount was shot out from under him. The man lay trapped beneath the horse as an Indian rushed at him with a raised war club. Carrington swung his horse toward the scene and got off several shots with his Colt. The Indian either fell or turned away; the colonel could not tell which.

Indian ponies enveloped his small group, and he ordered the soldiers to dismount and form into a circular defense. Gun barrels glistened in the pale December light as Carrington directed a steady stream of bullets into his attackers. He made certain that the men staggered their fire, which allowed every other trooper time to reload. Though they rarely appeared to hit either Indians or ponies, the hostiles could not break through.

Carrington finally turned to the bugler Metzger. The language barrier was not too great for the little German to understand Carrington's frantic demand to sound the bugle for recall. Metzger pursed his lips and blew for his life. The cracked notes carried on the cold wind and echoed off the hills and ridges, and the Indians inexplicably quit. Carrington turned to see his stragglers riding to his rescue. Moments later, Capt. Fetterman appeared from out of the timber with fourteen mounted infantrymen.

The colonel briefed Fetterman, informing him that Lieutenants Grummond and Bingham were missing. Col. Carrington guessed that they might be off near Peno Creek, and led the combined troop in that direction. They heard the drumming of hoofbeats before they saw the riders. Lt. Grummond and three enlisted men broke through the scrub oak, galloping straight for them. Seven screaming Indians were a few yards behind them. The Indians veered off, shaking their lances and war clubs as they vanished along the twisting trail.

Grummond, gulping air, reined in his steaming horse beside the colonel's, and the two seemed to shout at each other. What they said is not known, although Lt. Bisbee testified later that Grummond told him he had demanded to know if Carrington was a "coward or a fool" to allow his command to be cut to pieces.

It was then that Col. Carrington realized that he was still short an officer. When Lt. Grummond regained his composure, he told a troubling tale. He and Lt. Bingham were following the raiding party into the valley when hundreds of Indians streamed out of gullies and surrounded them. Grummond said he watched Bingham turn in his saddle, shout, "Come on," and gallop ahead with four men. But most of his raw, frightened troopers froze in their tracks in the face of the Indian onslaught.

A few had begun to turn their mounts to make a run for the fort when Grummond, Capt. Brown, and another officer leveled their guns to check the retreat. By the time they re-formed and scattered the Indians, Lt. Bingham had disappeared down a narrow, twisting trail that led to the flats along the frozen Peno Creek. Lt. Grummond rode after him alone. He caught him and his small patrol two miles away, stalking a single warrior. Then, he told Col. Carrington, he joined the hunt.

That lone Indian was Crazy Horse.

. . .

It may have struck Crazy Horse as too easy. Had these naive American officers never fought an Indian before? Red Cloud had taught his warriors to differentiate officers from enlisted men by the strange symbols they wore on their shoulders and sleeves and the long knives the officers carried at their sides. These two had simply taken his bait as if they were trout. Crazy Horse dismounted and pretended to examine his pony's hind leg, acting as if he were digging a stone from its hoof. On either side of him, he could see the puffs of vapor expelled from the mouths of his fellow Strong Hearts concealed in the shallow draws.

A soldier fired at him. Crazy Horse did not move. He allowed the little group of Bluecoats, six in all, to come close enough for one of them to draw his saber and charge. He leaped on his pony and rode hard. They followed. And then the Strong Hearts jumped from their hiding places and surrounded them. A gunshot sounded, shattering the face of the officer with the drawn saber.

Lt. Bingham slumped over his pommel and was yanked from the saddle. An Indian scalped him; another grabbed his horse. There were no more arrows or gunshots from the Indians. They wanted the horses. That was what saved the rest of the Bluecoats.

Except one. The Indians surrounded the little group and tried to lasso the soldiers and pull them off their mounts. Sgt. Gideon Bowers, a grizzled Civil War veteran, shot three warriors dead with his Colt before they pulled him to the ground. Indians swarmed him and hacked repeatedly with tomahawks and knives. In the fighting at close quarters, the

Sioux attempted to loop their bowstrings over the remaining four soldiers' heads. The enlisted men used the butt ends of their rifles as clubs, and Grummond slashed with his saber. He could hear a repulsive click with every skull he broke open.

Finally, he jammed the sword into his horse's neck. The animal reared up and kicked its forelegs, creating an opening. Grummond broke away and galloped back toward the ridge, the three enlisted men following him. Half a dozen Indians jumped onto their ponies and raced, screaming, after them. They quit the chase, however, at the sight of Col. Carrington's and Capt. Fetterman's column.

Then, suddenly, as if by magic, the Indians were gone. Patches of crusty snow up and down Lodge Trail Ridge were smeared with blood, which grew thicker at the site where Lt. Bingham and Bowers had fallen. The Indians had carried off their own dead. Col. Carrington ordered a search for the Americans' bodies, and within the hour they found Sgt. Bowers. Astonishingly, he was still alive. However, he died moments later. Not far away, Lt. Bingham was impaled on a tree stump, his body bristling with more than fifty arrow shafts. By midafternoon the troop was back at the post, where Carrington tried to make sense of the blunder-filled fight.

The cowardice of the inexperienced recruits was at least understandable, if still disgraceful. But Lt. Grummond had disobeyed a direct order and, for whatever reason, Lt. Bingham had abandoned his men to ride off recklessly to his death—and now the cavalry had no officers.

Even Capt. Fetterman was at a loss to explain the actions

of Lt. Bingham, a decorated Civil War commander. "I cannot account for this movement on the part of an officer of such unquestionable gallantry," he wrote in his report.

Given all that had gone wrong, it was a near miracle that Bingham and Bowers were the only men killed. Another sergeant and four privates had been wounded, and five horses had been so badly injured that they needed to be put down. More amazingly, Capt. Fetterman for once appeared chastened. "This Indian war has become a hand-to-hand fight," he told Col. Carrington when he delivered his written report. In his own dispatch, the colonel generously estimated that at least 10 Indians out of 300 attackers were killed, one by a bullet from his own Colt, and perhaps twice as many wounded.

Yet for Red Cloud it had been a dress rehearsal.

38

A Gathering Force

Red Cloud was convinced: these foolish soldiers were ready to be slaughtered. He had watched the previous day's fighting, and even directed some of it from a high peak in Peno Creek valley, marveling at the dull-witted behavior of the Bluecoats. They were like spoiled, ignorant children—dangle a piece of hard candy in front of them and they would do anything, no matter how stupid, to grab it.

Back at the Indian camp, Crazy Horse described the parts of the battle Red Cloud had not personally witnessed. The young warrior told of how he twice lured officers—first Bingham, then Grummond—away from their troops, as easily as separating an old cow from a buffalo herd. When Red Cloud summoned the Lakota subchief Yellow Eagle, who had led the initial attack on the wood train, Yellow Eagle boasted of baiting Fetterman's and Bingham's larger party and allowing them to ride past him while he lay in wait for the Little White Chief's smaller patrol.

If it had worked once, why not a second time with a larger force? Red Cloud consulted with his allies. The Miniconjou head men High Backbone and Black Shield agreed, as did the Cheyenne war chiefs Roman Nose and Medicine Man. Two Arapaho—Little Chief and Sorrel Horse—said their seventy-five braves were prepared to fight.

All told there were more than 2,000 warriors. Red Cloud decided that on the first favorable day after the next full moon the Lakota, Cheyenne, and Arapaho would ride south. They would again feint toward the soldiers' wood train, and again work the decoy trick along the ridge. But this time they would lure as many men as possible out of the fort, kill them all, and burn the American outpost.

In the two weeks following the December 6 fight, not a single hostile incident was recorded, although the Lakota scouts remained ever-present on distant hills, signaling with mirrors, smoke, and flags. The Indians appeared to be regrouping. In fact, 2,000 warriors were camped just over Lodge Trail Ridge.

The warriors had arrived that morning, a large war party consisting of Lakota, Cheyenne, and Arapaho. On the ride, they had observed the same formalities as before the attacks on Julesburg and Bridge Station: official Pipe Bearers rode ahead of Red Cloud and the other war chiefs leading the column, while Strong Hearts and Cheyenne Crazy Dogs kept discipline on its flanks.

They made camp about ten miles north of the American post, and following a brief skirmish with Capt. Powell's relief force that morning at the pinery, they dug in for the night. A snowstorm swept in on a bitter north wind, and by dawn on December 20 the snow was still falling, a feathery powder that blanketed the prairie. The head men agreed to postpone any more fighting for at least a day while their warriors put up small, mobile tepees in three abutting circles, one for each tribe.

They lit warming fires, and around midday a few hunting parties returned with fresh deer and buffalo meat, but it was not nearly enough to feed the entire camp, and most of the braves gnawed on hunks of frozen pemmican. Scouts were posted on the hills overlooking the fort. They reported that the weather had also kept most of the soldiers indoors.

Red Cloud and his fellow war leaders decided that the best place to ambush the soldiers was on the forks of Peno Creek, about halfway between the Indian camp and the American fort. They would trap the Americans on the flats of the little valley carved by the creek, attacking from the gullies and thickets dense enough to hide a large force.

But what if the soldiers refused to cross the Lodge Trail Ridge and ride down into the valley? That Powell's detachment had ignored the decoys after scattering the raiding party was worrisome. Perhaps the Americans were not as stupid as they looked.

As evening dissolved into night two, the weather turned again, and a warm breeze blew up from the Southern Plains to melt most of the snow, although it remained deep in the mountains and shaded gulches. It was decided at the council fire that the next morning would be a good day to fight.

The Battle Begins

December 21, 1866, dawned glorious, the sun bright. It was the kind of crisp morning that often follows a storm in the Powder River Country, with the air cold and dry and the wind still. It was a dramatic turn from the previous night's unseasonable warmth, and an indication of a colder storm front moving in.

Most of the snow around Fort Phil Kearny had melted, but Col. Carrington knew that it would still be deep in the pine forests. He delayed the wood train's morning departure until he was convinced that the weather would hold at least for the day.

Red Cloud was grateful for the snowmelt. His warriors could now hide themselves in the draws and ravines of the Peno Creek valley without leaving tracks. A mile-long section of the Bozeman Trail followed Peno Creek on a thin path connecting two buttes. This elevated route was known as the High Backbone, and its edges fell off steeply on either side into cutbanks thick with bushes and tall scrub. Red Cloud would position his force in these thickets, while Yellow Eagle would lead a smaller raiding party of perhaps forty warriors toward the fort's pinery; the soldiers might find that number more enticing to attack.

When Yellow Eagle departed, the Oglala, Cheyenne, and Arapaho formed up to the southwest of the High Backbone, and the bulk of the Miniconjous and a few scattered Sans Arcs concentrated below the path's bank on the northeast. Red Cloud and his battle chiefs rode about another quarter mile down the valley and climbed the tallest hill. From here, with a pair of his captured binoculars, Red Cloud could see both the ambush site and the wood train road winding toward the new bridge onto Piney Island.

At 10 a.m., Col. Carrington ordered the woodcutters to set out from the fort, this time with an extra guard attached to the usual mounted escort. There were perhaps ninety soldiers and civilians in the group, about double the usual number.

Less than an hour later, the lookouts on Pilot Knob waved their coded flags, signaling to the fort that a raiding party was attacking the wood train. They had spotted Yellow Eagle's decoy party. Bugles sounded inside the post as two Indians appeared above the fort across Big Piney Creek on the south slope of Lodge Trail Ridge. They dismounted, wrapped their red blankets tight about them, and sat beneath a lone serviceberry tree, watching the activity inside the log walls.

Col. Carrington was surprised when Capt. Fetterman arrived on the steps of his headquarters with fifty-three men. The colonel would later say that he had sent for Capt. Powell to lead the relief detail. But Capt. Fetterman reminded Col. Carrington that he outranked Powell in length of service, and asked to be the one to take out the relief group.

Carrington was in a bind. Men were under attack several miles up the road. He did not have time to waste arguing the finer points of command with his unruly number two. He allowed Capt. Fetterman to lead the group—but, he was to testify, not before issuing these orders to Fetterman: "Support the wood train. Relieve it and report to me. Do not engage or pursue Indians at its expense. Under no circumstances pursue over . . . Lodge Trail Ridge."

No one else heard Carrington give these orders.

Capt. Fetterman's infantry, flanked by the horsemen, had nearly reached the south gate of the fort when Carrington sent his aide running to intercept the captain and have him repeat the orders back. Fetterman allegedly did this before exiting the post. The colonel then summoned Lt. Grummond and directed him to muster the remainder of the cavalry and follow Fetterman up the road. The riders would undoubtedly overtake the marching infantry, and Grummond was to fall in with Fetterman's troop "and not leave him." Col. Carrington inspected Grummond's twenty-three cavalrymen, each outfitted with a rapid-fire Spencer rifle, and repeated the orders forbidding Lt. Grummond to cross Lodge Trail Ridge.

Before Lt. Grummond rode out, Capt. Brown and a private named Thomas Maddeon approached Col. Carrington. They asked to join the detail. Maddeon had somehow seized the last fit horse in the stables, and a jubilant Capt. Brown was leading a pony belonging to the colonel's young son. The colonel granted them permission and checked his pocket watch; it was nearly 11:30. Outside the post, the innkeeper James Wheatley and a miner, Isaac Fisher, fell in with the group, bringing it to twenty-seven men. These two civilians were former Union Army officers who apparently had a hankering to kill Indians and had just purchased new sixteen-shot Henry rifles.

Col. Carrington climbed the post's sentry walk and watched Capt. Fetterman veer off the wood road, cross Big Piney Creek, and turn onto a trail running west along the south slope of Lodge Trail Ridge—the same ascent he himself had made two weeks earlier during the fight on December 6. Col. Carrington suspected that Fetterman was about to disobey his orders and lead his troop over Lodge Trail Ridge. Confused and angry, he turned toward the sentries on Pilot Knob. They were signaling that the wood train was no longer fighting with the Indians and was rolling onto the pinery.

Col. Carrington knew that Capt. Fetterman, perhaps a mile from the post, could also see the flagmen, and he calmed down. He assumed that Fetterman had decided to reach the high ground in order to ambush the Indian raiding party from behind. By now Lt. Grummond's horsemen had caught up to Fetterman's foot soldiers, and together they climbed the slope.

Fetterman deployed guards on his flanks and, as Col. Carrington noticed, "was evidently moving wisely up the creek and along the southern slope of Lodge Trail Ridge, with good promise of cutting off the Indians as they should withdraw." The colonel also saw that Fetterman's position offered "perfect vantage ground" should the raiders turn and attack the wood train again.

Col. Carrington also noticed the two Indians huddled beneath the tree across Big Piney Creek. He ordered Capt. Powell to direct the artillerymen to lob caution shots toward them. Much to everyone's surprise, the whistling shell fragments forced another thirty Indians from the brushy gullies. The hostiles fled back up the ridge. One pony was riderless.

It was with a sense of relief that Col. Carrington, "entertaining no further thought of danger," climbed down from the bastion. Capt. Fetterman and Lt. Grummond were apparently obeying his command to engage only the war party that had attacked the wood train, and his big guns had scattered any hostile rear guard. He walked back to his headquarters, he would later write, with his mind already elsewhere, contemplating the final touches he would put on his post.

By noon Lt. Grummond's cavalry was slightly outpacing Capt. Fetterman's infantry, and had ridden about halfway up the slope of Lodge Trail Ridge. Grummond halted his men just below the site where the Bozeman Trail ran northwest through a cut in the ridgeline, to wait for Fetterman.

The sky had darkened, and against the skyline Lt. Grummond could make out individual braves, perhaps ten, racing their ponies near the crest. They waved red blankets to try to frighten his horses, and their wolflike yips and howls echoed off the buttes and hills rising from Big Piney Creek. Within moments Capt. Fetterman's force had caught up to Grummond, and he ordered a volley fired at the bold savages. The

Indians rode their ponies out of rifle range, but before the gun smoke cleared they had danced back and were daring the soldiers to chase them farther up the incline. Among them was Crazy Horse.

Capt. Fetterman continued climbing in skirmish formation, but he was hesitant. Below the crest of the ridge, he held his position for a good twenty minutes. The lookouts on Pilot Knob who were tracking his advance signaled to the post that he had halted the troop. Fetterman knew that the wood train he had been sent to protect was safe. To support the wood train had been the colonel's primary directive. That had been accomplished. With the wood train safe, he could now either turn back toward the post, or teach the Indians a hard lesson about fighting "real" soldiers. It was Crazy Horse who forced his hand.

The wispy brave with wavy hair dashed to and fro before the Bluecoats on his favorite reddish-brown racing horse, distinguished by its white face and stockings. He tried every trick he knew. He taunted the soldiers in English with vile curses. He dismounted within rifle range, again pretending that his horse had pulled up lame. He waved his blanket and stood tall with obvious disdain as bullets pocked the dirt at his feet. He even dismounted and started a small fire, acting as if his horse was so injured that he had given up.

Still Capt. Fetterman would not budge. Crazy Horse, clad in only a breechclout and deerskin leggings, with a single hawk's feather twined in his hair and a lone pebble tied behind his ear for good luck, was down to his final ploy. He turned his back toward the soldiers, flipped his breechclout up over his back, pulled down his leggings, and wiggled his naked bum in their faces.

The sentries on Pilot Knob shifted their binoculars from the taunting Indian to Capt. Fetterman, who was pacing before his infantrymen. They saw him unsheathe his saber and appear to shout. The lookouts blinked, and the soldiers were gone.

40

Decoy to
Destruction

When Capt. Fetterman's foot soldiers
reached the butte where the path of the High Backbone
began, they started crossing it, firing as they walked. A few
taunting Indians fell.

Meanwhile, Lt. Grummond's cavalry, descending the
ridge in front of Capt. Fetterman and several hundred yards
to his left, spotted what appeared to be a small Indian village
farther down Peno Creek, perhaps half a mile to the northwest. Without consulting Fetterman he ordered a charge,
and the cavalry spurred their horses into a gallop. The civilians Wheatley and Fisher led the way with five additional
troopers.

At a few minutes past noon, Crazy Horse and his decoys
skidded their horses across the ice of Peno Creek and out
of rifle range, with the infantry still marching after them.
Suddenly the Indians halted, formed two single files, and
streamed back toward the whites. Not far from the creek the

two lines crossed in a perfect X. This move was a prearranged signal to the hidden war party.

Two thousand warriors rose as one. A war cry echoed through the hills, a curdling scream evoked by half a century of white indignities, lies, and betrayals. The Indians rolled toward the soldiers like a prairie fire. From the left, Cheyenne horsemen charged from clusters of dogwoods and cottonwoods. From the right, Lakota and Arapaho on foot scrambled from the tall grass and shot out from behind ash and box elders. Arrows blackened the sky, killing and wounding both friend and foe. Capt. Fetterman's commands could barely be heard amid the shrieks and whistles.

Back at the fort, Col. Carrington climbed to a lookout station on top of his quarters. At the sound of distant gunfire, he scanned the ridgeline with his binoculars. He saw neither soldiers nor Indians. The colonel had received word from the woodcutters that they had reached the blockhouses on Piney Island with no casualties, but he knew that an Indian raiding party was still lurking somewhere between the fort and the sawmill.

No one at the post was alarmed by either the gunshots or Capt. Fetterman's disappearance from view. Hostiles would not dare attack so strong a force—"the largest," the new arrival Lieutenant Wilbur Arnold noted, "that had ever been sent out from the garrison."

Col. Carrington assumed that his officers had decided to clear out the decoys near Peno Creek before coming back over the northernmost crest of the ridge and flanking the war party near the pinery. It was what he would have done;

it was what he had attempted to do on December 6.

He was slightly concerned that both Capt. Fetterman and Lt. Grummond had disregarded his orders not to cross the ridge, but he understood the necessity of making tactical decisions in the field. As a precaution, he directed Capt. Ten Eyck to assemble a group that would march to the sound of the rifle reports. Ten Eyck gathered the last forty infantrymen with working weapons and reported to the colonel.

Carrington told him that after he merged with Capt. Fetterman's troop, all soldiers were to return to the post. Capt. Ten Eyck's infantrymen marched out quickly, but were slowed while fording Big Piney Creek. The ice had partially melted and had not completely refrozen, and the men removed their socks and boots to wade across. At the creek, a handful of mounted civilians fell in next to them.

Meanwhile, Col. Carrington called for what was left of the cavalry and ordered the teamster wagon masters to gather all armed civilians still at the post. The group came to about thirty men, and some of these piled into three mule-drawn ammunition wagons and an ambulance in order to catch up to Capt. Ten Eyck. This meant there were no more serviceable horses at the fort.

Capt. Fetterman somehow managed to form up his surrounded troops and marched them back across the High Backbone through the rain of arrows until they reached a pile of flat rocks atop the butte. From there they could go no farther. The air soured with powder smoke as Fetterman ordered his men into two loose, outward-facing skirmish lines twenty paces apart. This was a formation ideal in Civil War battles to determine an enemy's position and provide cover for larger forces or reinforcements. But there were no reinforcements within striking distance, and these tactics meant little to the marauding Indians.

Far below Capt. Fetterman in the Peno Creek valley, Lt. Grummond realized too late what had happened. As he neared the village, he too was nearly enveloped by warriors; his stunned cavalrymen reined in their panicked, rearing mounts, awaiting orders that would never come. Grummond and a veteran sergeant were among the first to fall dead.

The cavalry retreated in terror, ignoring Capt. Fetterman's plight and making for the crest of Lodge Trail Ridge. They also abandoned the civilians Wheatley and Fisher and the little patrol of point riders, who were too far out in front and were quickly cut off. This latter group dismounted and formed a small circle; the concentrated fire from their guns felled so many braves that within moments a great pile of dead Indians and ponies, mixed with their own slain animals, formed a natural barricade. But there were too many Indians. They kept coming until it was knives and tomahawks against bayonets and swinging rifle butts.

Back at the rock pile, Capt. Fetterman was also fast losing soldiers. His skirmish lines had broken up into two loosely concentric rings rapidly collapsing in on themselves—a tightening noose with the captain in its center. Their position at the top of the rise bought them some time, but daring Indians burst through the defenses on horse and on foot, first singly, then by twos and threes, and finally a second storm of arrows preceded a wave of thrusting lances and swinging war clubs. Warriors in front were pushed ahead by a surge from behind. The soldiers fired their old guns, but the Indians were so close that there was no time to reload.

Capt. Brown broke away from the surviving cavalry troops who were scrambling up Lodge Trail Ridge and somehow made it through the mass of bodies at the rock pile. He dismounted beside his friend Capt. Fetterman, set loose Jimmy Carrington's pony, and stood back-to-back with his old commander, shooting. Brown fought off one charging Indian while another, a Lakota named American Horse, rushed his war pony into the rocks and hit Fetterman in the head with his club. American Horse leaped from his saddle onto Fetterman's body and killed him.

The dwindling infantry fought hand to hand, some from their knees, swinging their shattered rifles. When several soldiers broke from the rocks and made a run for the cavalry, Indians sprinted after them.

Capt. Brown was still standing, surrounded by carnage, both white and Indian. He had one cartridge left in his revolver. He put the barrel to his temple and pulled the trigger.

Meanwhile, up on the slope of Lodge Trail Ridge, the frantic, terrified cavalrymen led their horses by the reins. The climb across the icy hollows of the boulder-strewn hillside was slow and hard, and some horses skittered and broke away. One man walked backward, a lonesome rear guard continuously pumping the lever of his seven-shot Spencer rifle, reloading, and firing again. The few infantrymen who

This illustration, which appeared in *Harper's Weekly*, shows the artist's impression of the Fetterman Massacre. *Library of Congress*

had escaped the rock pile rushed past him up the incline. He covered them until an arrow tore through his heart.

When the first cavalrymen reached the summit—a narrow, slippery forty-foot shelf—they could see Fort Phil Kearny less than four miles away on the plateau beyond Big Piney Creek. They also saw Yellow Eagle's raiders, reinforced with at least 100 braves, charging up the south slope on snorting war ponies. The troopers' escape was blocked. They released their horses and dug into a cluster of boulders.

There was a lull in the battle cries, and for a moment the Americans dared to hope that reinforcements had overtaken the war party. The Indians had indeed broken off the attack, but only to collect the army horses. A shower of arrows signaled their return.

Now Indian spotters watching the fort flashed mirror signals to Red Cloud that more soldiers—Capt. Ten Eyck's group—were crossing Big Piney Creek. This news was at first greeted eagerly, but then the scouts signaled that the soldiers were riding in wagons. Red Cloud was certain this meant the soldiers were hauling artillery. He knew that even carrying heavy howitzers, the soldiers would crest the ridge in less than thirty minutes. Was that enough time to kill every last white still caught in the ambush?

Red Cloud signaled back from the tall hill, and the warriors surrounding the cavalry crawled as close as they could to the boulders. At a second signal they stood and ran, vanishing in clouds of Bluecoat gun smoke. The Indians suffered heavy casualties as they jabbed their lances and swung their war clubs and tomahawks, scalping soldiers alive. Crazy

Horse was said to have been among these fighters, killing with his steel hatchet.

The German bugler Adolph Metzger was one of the last to die. He found a crevasse between two large rocks, burrowed in backward, and fired his Spencer until its magazine was empty. Then he swung his bugle until it was a shapeless hunk of metal smeared with blood and war paint. It was said that for his bravery, he was accorded the highest honor his enemies could bestow—he was not scalped, unlike all the other soldiers. His bleeding, battered body, wounded in a dozen places, was covered with a buffalo-robe as a sign of respect.

If this is true, Metzger was the exception. The official army report, suppressed for twenty years, noted that many of the soldiers were probably still alive when they were scalped and mutilated. From decoy to destruction, it had taken the Indians a mere forty minutes to wipe out Capt. Fetterman's command. Eighty-one Americans lay dead.

41

Like Hogs
Brought to Market

On the southern slope of Lodge Trail Ridge,
Capt. Ten Eyck and his men heard the firing on the other
side of the ridge grow louder. But instead of following Capt.
Fetterman's path directly up the Bozeman Trail, Ten Eyck
ordered his troops east and then north, aiming for the ridgeline's highest point. He wanted to be certain he controlled
the high ground for whatever he would face on the other side
of the crest. The route added fifteen to twenty minutes to his
mission.

At 12:45, Capt. Ten Eyck's lead riders were just topping
the ridge some 200 yards east of the battlefield, when all gunshots from the Peno Creek valley ceased. One of the civilians
riding just ahead of Ten Eyck's troop thought he heard groans
and screams. Within minutes, the entire column had reached
the summit.

The Peno Creek valley stretching before them was filled
with thousands of painted warriors, more than any man in

the garrison had ever seen. Many seemed to be concentrated on either side of the High Backbone. When the Indians spotted the relief detail they jeered, shrieked, and waved their weapons toward the sky, daring the Americans to come down and fight. Others were running down saddled American horses and recovering some of the 40,000 arrows that had been shot, 1,000 for every minute of the fight. Still others were loading their dead onto makeshift travois or tending to their wounded. And a group of about a hundred were clustered around a pile of boulders half a mile or so to the west along the crest of the ridgeline.

Capt. Ten Eyck was confused. Where was Capt. Fetterman's infantry? Where was Lt. Grummond's cavalry? He dispatched his only mounted messenger back to the fort and continued to stare at the vista before him, trying to make sense of what he was seeing. When his wagons arrived, the Indians, fearing that they were hauling howitzers, slowly withdrew from the little valley. Suddenly a trooper cried, "There're the men down there, all dead."

From a distance the white, naked bodies could have been mistaken for patches of snow.

Back at the fort, Col. Carrington paced his small lookout tower, watching as Captain Ten Eyck's relief party topped the ridge. Below him, on the front porch, Mrs. Wheatley and the wives of officers and enlisted men gathered with the colonel's wife, Margaret Carrington. The women stared wordlessly at the heights across the Big Piney. "The silence," wrote Frances Grummond, who was five months pregnant, "was dreadful."

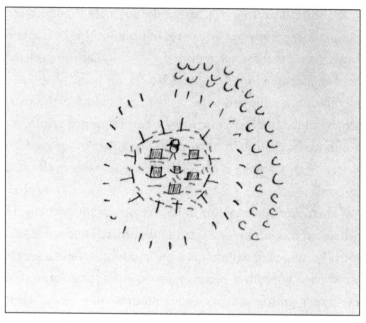

This illustration of the battle of December 21, 1866, created by the Sioux brave American Horse, depicts U.S. Army soldiers surrounded on Massacre Ridge. *Courtesy National Anthropological Archives, Smithsonian Institution*

At a little past one o'clock they spotted a lone horse-man, Capt. Ten Eyck's messenger, riding furiously down the slope. Within moments, he had galloped through the main gate and skidded to a halt before the colonel's headquarters. "Captain Ten Eyck says he can see or hear nothing of Captain Fetterman," the courier reported. "The Indians are on the road challenging him to come down."

There were Indians as far as the eye could see, the mes-senger added, and Capt. Ten Eyck had requested reinforce-ments and a mountain howitzer. Then the man lowered his voice. "The Captain is afraid Fetterman's party is all gone up, sir."

There were no more fit horses to replace the messenger's exhausted mount, so Col. Carrington ordered one of his per-sonal horses, a big, sturdy gray, retrieved from the stable. He scrawled a note on a piece of paper, informing Capt. Ten Eyck that reinforcements and ammunition were on their way. And as if doubting either the captain or his messenger, he also ordered Ten Eyck to find Fetterman, unite with him, collect the wood train, and return to the post.

Up on the Lodge Trail Ridge, Capt. Ten Eyck waited until the entire huge war party had departed over a string of dis-tant buttes before he advanced cautiously down the north slope. He reached Peno Creek and turned west, following the wagon ruts of the Bozeman Trail. The knoll with the flat-topped rock pile loomed before him. Bodies covered the stones. The corpses formed a ring about forty feet in diame-ter. The harsh wind had scattered much paper—maps, unsent letters, journal pages—a common sight in the aftermath of frontier warfare. Some soldiers recognized fellow infantrymen from scraps of uniforms that the Indians had not shredded or stolen.

It was difficult to identify individuals, although "Bald Head Eagle" (Brown), with a powder burn on his temple and a bullet in his brain, was recognizable. He was the only trooper killed by a gunshot and the Indians had scalped his bald spot. Dead Indian ponies and American horses littered the ground. In the cuts and draws below, on the rises above, and in the scrub and among the trees, they found more soldiers—scalped, mutilated, the blood freezing in their wounds. They had yet to discover Lt. Grummond's troops on the ridge.

The temperature was falling, and the corpses were rapidly stiffening. Capt. Ten Eyck ordered as many bodies loaded into the four wagons as could fit. It was rough, slow work, and they did not reach the gates of Fort Phil Kearny until dusk. "We brought in about fifty in wagons," wrote the post surgeon, "like you see hogs brought to market."

As night fell the temperature dropped below zero, the wind picked up, and Fort Phil Kearny was locked down and braced for the next attack. Nearly a third of its garrison had abruptly vanished. Col. Carrington sent for the armed soldiers and teamsters still on Piney Island. He also ordered all civilians brought into the fort, released every prisoner from the guardhouse, and placed the entire post under arms.

The howitzers and mounds of grapeshot were pulled to the battlements, rifles were stacked across the parade ground, and orders were passed to bar every door and window. Three troopers were assigned to each of the stockade's firing loop-holes, but most of the long-range rifles had been captured in the fight. Ammunition was so short that each man was issued only five rounds. Every man understood that the fort could not hold out long against a full-on assault.

When the wagons arrived from the pinery, Col. Carrington had the beds removed and upended to form three concentric circles securing the post's underground ammunition magazine. As he studied the Indian signal fires on the hills and ridges around the fort, his wife knocked on Frances Grummond's door to break the news that her husband was still missing. Given the "horrible and sickening" condition of the forty-nine bodies carried back to the post—these were being sorted through and identified in the emptied guardhouse—neither woman held much hope that he was still alive. Margaret Carrington insisted that the lieutenant's wife move into her quarters, and as Frances gathered a few belongings, another knock sounded on her door. She pulled it open to find a dark, wiry civilian with a pointy black beard and "bright, piercing eyes" filling the small doorframe.

Mrs. Grummond knew this man's name, although they had never before spoken to each other. He was John "Portugee" Phillips, the mining partner of Isaac Fisher. Phillips had been born to Portuguese parents, and in a lilting accent he told her that he had been out hauling water when Fisher and Wheatley joined her husband's troop, or else he would have surely ridden with them. Now, he said, Col. Carrington had called for volunteers to ride to Fort Laramie for help, and he had stepped forward. He had come, he said, to say good-bye.

Frances Grummond was flustered. She barely knew the man.

John Phillips glanced at Mrs. Grummond's swollen belly. "I will go if it costs me my life," he said with tears in his eyes. And though still in shock and taken somewhat aback by the stranger's familiarity, she finally understood his words to mean that Phillips was following his own code of the West, whereby the safety of a pregnant woman in danger was paramount. Phillips removed the wolf-skin robe from his shoulders and handed it to her before departing. "I brought it for you to keep and remember me by if you never see me again," he said. Then he turned and left.

Throughout all this—the preparations for an attack, the identification of the bodies stacked in the guardhouse, the mourning, the fear and confusion—memories of Capt. William Judd Fetterman and his eighty dead hovered over the little outpost like ghosts. No one slept well that night.

Col. Carrington hunched over his lamp-lit writing desk and scratched out two messages: one for Gen. Cooke in Omaha and one for Gen. Grant in Washington. He described what little he knew of the day's battle—"a fight unexampled in Indian warfare"—and informed his superiors that though only forty-nine bodies had been recovered, he suspected that the missing thirty-one troopers and their officer, Lt. Grummond, were also dead.

Without immediate reinforcements armed with Spencer rifles, he wrote, an avenging "expedition now with my force is impossible." He assured both generals that he was prepared to defend Fort Phil Kearny to the last man, and concluded with this: "The Indians are desperate; I spare none, and they spare none."

It must have occurred to Col. Carrington that the army and the country would soon be looking for someone to blame. It was likely with this in mind that he added a personal comment to Gen. Grant's dispatch: "I think you should know the facts at once. . . . I want men. . . . I will operate all winter, whatever the season, if supported; but to redeem my pledge to open and guarantee this [territory], I must have re-enforcements and the best of arms."

Carrington had his aide make two copies of both letters. In addition to Phillips, he recruited two more couriers—a miner named William Bailey and the wagon master George Dillon—to ride separately to Horseshoe Station, the closest telegraph office, 196 miles away. But the Horseshoe Station line was frequently down, so, if it was, he instructed all three to continue on to Fort Laramie, another 40 miles south. It was Phillips in whom he had the most confidence.

It was nearing midnight on December 21 when Col. Carrington met Phillips in the quartermaster's stables. He led Phillips to his own stalls, where the miner selected one of the colonel's personal horses, a white Kentucky thoroughbred. Phillips crammed the saddlebags with hardtack and tied a quarter-sack of oats to his pommel.

The thermometer read eighteen degrees below zero, and the air smelled of a gathering storm. Phillips cinched his buffalo-fur coat, wrapped tight the wool leggings beneath his thigh-high buffalo boots, pulled his beaver hat low over his ears, and jammed his hands into sheepskin mittens that

John Phillips (left) and Capt. James Powell survived
the fighting at Fort Phil Kearny in 1866. Phillips
endured an exhausting journey through blizzards and
bitter cold to report the Fetterman massacre.
*Courtesy American Heritage Center, University of
Wyoming*

stretched to his elbows. He then led the horse to the southeast water gate of the quartermaster's yard, Col. Carrington walking beside him. The first threatening bits of swirling sleet and snow pricked the men's faces.

The three enlisted men posted at the gate were jumpy. At the sound of boots crunching on the frozen ground, a private called out a challenge. Col. Carrington moved close enough to be recognized and the sergeant of the guard shouted, "Attention!"

"Never mind, sergeant," Col. Carrington said. "Open the gate."

Two soldiers pushed open the heavy log doors and stood silent. Col. Carrington gave Phillips brief final instructions before reaching out to shake his hand. "May God help you," he said, and the horseman led his charger out, mounted, wheeled, and trotted away.

Col. Carrington and the three guardsmen stood wordless for half a minute, the colonel's head cocked as if he was listening for the hiss of an arrow. Then the hoofbeats went silent. "Good," he said. "He has taken softer ground at the side of the trail."

The snow began falling harder.

42

Fear and Mourning

The next morning, Col. Carrington's wife and his four surviving junior officers tried to talk him out of it but the colonel insisted. He would not allow the hostiles to sense any weakness. But the more powerful reason was that he had to see for himself. It was bitterly cold on December 22 when he mounted the sturdy gray he had lent to Capt. Ten Eyck's messenger twenty-four hours earlier. Eighty-three soldiers and civilians, the best he could select, followed him through the front gate toward Lodge Trail Ridge. Storm clouds moved down from the north, and enough spitting snow had already fallen to muffle the footfalls of the marchers and the creaking of the mule-drawn wagons.

When the bugler blew reveille and the report of the morning gun echoed back from the hills earlier that morning, Col. Carrington had expected the sound to be met with howls, eagle whistles, and arrows. But as the pale sun rose farther over Pilot Knob, not an Indian was visible on the ridges and hills. This, the colonel knew, did not mean the Indians were not there. It was, however, unlike them to refrain from exhibiting their joy at the outcome of the previous day's fight. Perhaps the reason was the blizzard that everyone sensed was coming.

While his troop assembled, Col. Carrington had whispered to Frances Grummond a promise to retrieve her husband's body. Then he gave Capt. Powell two orders. Capt. Ten Eyck would be accompanying him over the ridgeline, leaving Powell in charge of the post.

The first order concerned communications. On his departure, Carrington wrote, Powell was to run a white lamp up the flagstaff; if Indians appeared, he was to fire the twelve-pounder three times and substitute a red lantern for the white one. The second directive was more confidential, and Carrington pulled Powell aside to tell him in a whisper: "If in my absence," he said, "Indians in overwhelming numbers attack, put the women and children in the magazine with supplies of water, bread, crackers, and other supplies that seem best, and, in the event of a last desperate struggle, destroy all together, rather than have any captured alive."

To remove any doubt, the colonel himself strode through the circular wagon fortification, pulled open the magazine door, cut open a barrel of gunpowder, and laid a train of black powder that would ignite at the touch of a match.

Old Jim Bridger had hauled himself out of bed that morning and limped out into the day. Despite the intense pain in his arthritic joints, he had volunteered to ride as a scout. He, too, expected an attack at any moment, and he'd decided that when it occurred, it would be as fine an occasion as any to end his career and his life.

Once through the main gate, Bridger set about directing infantrymen to key sites and positioned pairs of soldiers on successive outcrops and ridges, creating a chain that reached all the way back to the fort. He made certain that each set of the guards standing higher and higher along the route would never be out of sight of the men below.

The temperature remained around zero, and darker storm clouds blotted out the sun as the detail trod silently past the rock pile where Capt. Fetterman's infantry had met their demise, and reached the high ground strewn with boulders that had barely sheltered Lt. Grummond's cavalry. The rocky earth along the ridgeline was streaked with frozen pools of blood, and the bodies of the horse soldiers were so stiff that one civilian likened the task of loading them onto the wagons to stacking firewood.

The men on the ridge, like Capt. Fetterman's soldiers, had been butchered, but other cavalrymen in the detail also recognized infantry insignia mixed among the dead.

From the ridgeline the wagons rolled slowly down to Peno Creek, where the body of Lt. Grummond was discovered.

A few hundred yards down the creek bed lay the bodies of James Wheatley, Isaac Fisher, "and four or five of the old, long-tried, and experienced soldiers." Piles of rifle cartridges littered the little ring created by their slain horses and an additional ten dead ponies. Outside the defensive circle a soldier counted sixty-five smudges of blood, perhaps indicating where an Indian had fallen.

It was dark before the column moved back over the crest of Lodge Trail Ridge. Excited word was passed from front to back that the white lantern still swung from the top of the flagstaff. There had been no Indian sightings. Back inside the fort, Col. Carrington handed Frances Grummond a sealed envelope containing a lock of her husband's hair from a portion that had not been scalped.

Not long afterward, the blizzard that had threatened all day began. The temperature dropped to twenty below zero, and by daylight on December 23, snowdrifts had crested so high against the west wall of the stockade that guards could walk over it. Jim Bridger assured Col. Carrington that not even Red Cloud was bold or crazy enough to attack in such weather. Even so, all through the day before Christmas, Fort Phil Kearny was tense. A triple guard remained at every loophole.

Col. Carrington dispatched a grave-digging detail to break the frozen earth beneath Pilot Knob. He hoped for a solemn Christmas Day service. But the snow was too high, the ground was too hard, and the threat of another attack was too overwhelming to spare enough men to complete the task. So a day late, on December 26, forty-two pine boxes were hurriedly covered with loose dirt in a shallow, fifty-foot-long trench. No words were spoken over the graves.

Following the somber ceremony, there was nothing to do but batten down Fort Phil Kearny and wait. For what, only God and Red Cloud knew.

. . .

The blizzard gave the Indians time to mourn. For three days the wives, sisters, mothers, and daughters in the great village on the Tongue River made their way to the bluffs to cut their fingers and arms and chop their hair in memory of the dead. Snowdrifts five and six feet deep ran red with blood. And then, on the fourth day, the victory dances commenced to celebrate the fight the Indians would come to call the Battle of the Hundred in the Hands.

Songs of praise were sung for Yellow Eagle for leading the raids on the wood road, and decoys such as Young Man Afraid of His Horses and American Horse, Capt. Fetterman's slayer, were celebrated at feasts. Crazy Horse was dragged into the firelight and for once not allowed to back away. He received honors for his deft disciplining of the decoy party, and old men sang of the fearlessness he had shown while standing unflinching against the American guns.

And then there was Red Cloud. To him went "all the honor" for the stunning victory. His strategic planning, so often questioned, had proved brilliant. Everything he had foreseen over the years, from the victory at Bridge Station to what he had warned in his verbal explosion at Fort Laramie, had occurred. He had held together his Indian coalition while balancing older, more experienced voices urging accommodation with the whites against young warriors too eager to strike too soon.

His forward thinking and his keen military judgment in choosing lieutenants such as Crazy Horse had filled the separate tribes with a sense of unity. He told his people that their cause, his cause, was just, and that the Black Hills, what the Sioux call *Paha Sapa*, or the Heart of Everything That Is, was worth fighting for and, if need be, dying for. Best of all, in the end it was the Bluecoats who had done the dying.

At the grand celebrations that followed the Peno Creek fight, Red Cloud's political rivals, Old Man Afraid of His Horses in particular, deferred to him. He graciously returned their praise while modestly accepting the accolades.

If Red Cloud seemed subdued, there was good reason. He fretted that his warriors had failed to destroy the despised fort between the Piney Creeks. And he knew that this war was far from over. The Battle of the Hundred in the Hands had been a fine start, perhaps even a signal to the Americans that they should leave the Powder River Country and never return.

But Red Cloud knew his enemy. The Americans would be back, and he would fight them again—and only on his terms. He also understood the ways of his own people and the allied tribes. Despite the victory, it would be difficult to rally them again so soon. His braves needed time to fill their bellies over warm winter fires, and the war ponies needed to recover their strength. It would be a short cold winter, and when the new grass sprouted from the prairie, he would reveal his next step.

Already the details were forming in his mind, like puzzle pieces clicking into place, locking in his next moves. First he would simultaneously attack the two most northern garrisons, Forts Phil Kearny and C. F. Smith, and kill everyone in them. That would leave Reno Station isolated, and either the army would abandon it or he would burn it. This was an audacious plan, but Red Cloud was certain it would work.

What to do about Fort Laramie, Red Cloud was not certain. By then the Americans might well have left the territory forever. In either case, he was certain of the eventual outcome. The Indian would prevail. Then, after it was all over, after Red Cloud had won his war, he would find rest in his lodge.

43

News of the Massacre

John Phillips rode by night, hiding by day, through one of the most vicious storms ever recorded on the High Plains. Somewhere along the trail, he met up with William Bailey and George Dillon. The three arrived late Christmas morning at Horseshoe Station, exhausted, hungry, and freezing. Bailey and Dillon were too spent to go on.

John Friend, the telegraph operator, tapped out a synopsis of Col. Carrington's dispatches. But he told the three messengers that he had received no telegraphs that day, and he feared that either the storm or the Indians had cut the line. Without saying a word, Phillips began rebinding his legs with burlap sacks to prepare for the ride to Fort Laramie.

Bailey and Dillon, collapsed in a heap by the fire, begged Phillips not to risk it. He ignored them, threw on his buffalo coat and beaver cap, saddled his horse, and disappeared into the whiteness. By noon the blizzard had blown north, behind him, and he traveled all afternoon beneath a bright sun reflecting the snow; by dusk he was snow-blind. Sunset brought relief but also the arrival of another storm. He rode by feel, always tracking south, the new sheets of snow thicker with his horse's every footfall.

The temperature was twenty-five degrees below zero when Phillips and his horse reeled through the main gate of Fort Laramie late on Christmas night. A ball was in progress, and he heard the strains of music as he slumped in his saddle and fell from his horse. Snow and ice matted his pointy black beard. Icicles hung from his coat and hat. The officer of the guard, a young lieutenant, rushed from his sentry box and helped him to his feet. Phillips was too weak to walk by himself, and his vocal cords were so frozen that his voice was a tinny croak when he said he needed to see the post's commanding officer.

The lieutenant slung Phillips's arm over his shoulders and half carried him to the ballroom, where the officers were about to select partners for the next dance. People gasped when he staggered through the door. The band fell silent and Lt. Col. Innis Palmer, Fort Laramie's commanding officer, rushed to his side. Earlier that afternoon, Lt. Col. Palmer had received a telegram from Horseshoe Station reporting an Indian massacre. But the communication was so garbled and incomplete—it did not say who had been massacred, or where the incident had occurred—that he took it as just another of the many rumors that flew across the High Plains.

Now Phillips reached under his buffalo coat and woolen shirts and pulled out Col. Carrington's dispatches. Lt. Col. Palmer's face whitened as he read them. He looked at Phillips, who had just ridden 236 miles in four days through raging blizzards—a feat that would become equal in western lore to Paul Revere's famous ride.

Palmer handed the messages to an aide, who ran to the post's telegraph office, and directed two soldiers to carry Phillips to the post infirmary. On the way, they passed Col. Carrington's white Kentucky thoroughbred charger, lying dead from exhaustion on the parade ground.

The Fort Laramie telegraph operator relayed the messages word for word to both Gen. Cooke in Omaha and Gen. Grant in Washington. It was 3:15 p.m. on December 26, 1866, when Gen. Grant and the War Department received the first news about what would soon be known nationwide as the Fetterman massacre.

The next morning, the *New York Times* provided brief details of the "horrid massacre" in the distant Dakota Territory, noting that it accounted for 8 percent of all army deaths in half a century of Indian fighting west of the Mississippi. And though what would later be referred to as Red Cloud's War was far from over, this was the moment when Gen. Grant came to the realization that the United States had been defeated for the first time by an Indian opponent.

Red Cloud never spoke to any whites of his great victory, so we are left to imagine his thoughts as the Bad Faces led the Lakota push west into the Bighorn Valley that winter. Perhaps he recalled his orphaned childhood, or his first lethal coup against the Pawnee. What we do know is that the boy shunned by so many and the man feared by all had

Red Cloud in a suit and tie in a formal portrait taken in 1891 when he was seventy years old. *Library of Congress*

accomplished what no other Indian ever had before.

The son of an alcoholic Brule had taught himself to lead, to suppress his snarl and his personal rage and remain still when he wanted to strike out. He had developed a steely self-discipline, and it had enabled him to become the first warrior chief to transform an Indian military culture that had stood for centuries. He had not only united the Lakota, enticing Oglalas, Brules, Miniconjous, and Sans Arcs to fight as one, but had also drawn to his cause the Cheyenne, Arapaho, Nez Percé, and Shoshones. It was the only way, he knew from the beginning, to humble a people so strong, so numerous, so intent on taking his land when they already had so much of their own. And it was the only way to defeat them.

Broken Promises

If Red Cloud's fame was not already established throughout the United States—though it certainly was among whites on the frontier—the Battle of the Hundred in the Hands secured it.

After picking up details of the battle from smaller western newspapers, reporters and editors from St. Louis to the Eastern Seaboard presented to their shocked readers explicit and often incorrect reports of the fight and its aftermath.

Though far from accurate, these reports got the army's attention. In his annual report to Gen. Grant regarding "operations within my command," Gen. Sherman lamented that the army had failed "to follow the savages and take a just vengeance" for the Fetterman massacre. Behind the scenes, however, officials from the Bureau of Indian Affairs were already putting out treaty feelers to Red Cloud through more manageable Lakota like Spotted Tail. They were met with silence.

The U.S. government peace commission at Fort Laramie in 1867 hoped to negotiate an end to what became known as "Red Cloud's War." *Courtesy American Heritage Center, University of Wyoming*

William Tecumseh Sherman, 1868. *Library of Congress*

As soon as the first spring grass of 1867 began to nourish Indian ponies, Red Cloud's harassment of the three American forts in the Powder River Country began again.

As he had planned all along, Red Cloud returned to the environs of Fort Phil Kearny in June 1867 to begin a series of vicious skirmishes with the troops of the new commander of the fort. The post had been resupplied and there were fresh herds of cattle and horses to raid.

In late July, the war chiefs from the tribal alliance convened, and Red Cloud and the other Big Bellies laid plans to attack two of the white man's forts almost simultaneously. On the morning of August 1, a large war party of Cheyenne led by Dull Knife and Two Moons surrounded a civilian hay-cutting group protected by nineteen soldiers about two miles from Montana's Fort C. F. Smith. Two troopers and a civilian were killed as the Americans withstood a daylong assault. It was only when howitzers from the post arrived near dusk that the Cheyenne retreated with scores of captured army horses.

The next morning, August 2, a loaded wood train and its army escort set off from Piney Island for Fort Phil Kearny, and at about the same time an empty wood train consisting of fourteen wagons left the post for the pinery. Among the civilians working in the latter detail was John Phillips. All of the soldiers in the field were under the command of Capt. James Powell, who, along with Capt. Tenedor Ten Eyck, was a holdover from Col. Carrington's command.

Red Cloud, leading about 1,000 Oglala and Miniconjou warriors, climbed a high hill west of the fort to observe the action. Red Cloud was unaware that only a few weeks earlier, the garrison at Fort Phil Kearny had received a shipment of 700 new Springfield Allin Conversion rifles, along with 100,000 rounds of ammunition. This time, the Indians would not be fighting soldiers who had only outdated muzzle-loaders.

In overwhelming numbers they charged the makeshift pen, called a corral, on horseback and on foot; this was perhaps the only time in the history of the West that an Indian attack involved sacrificing a large number of lives in order to take a position. They absorbed the volley they were expecting and assumed they had the usual thirty seconds to swoop in while soldiers reloaded. Instead, they were shocked and repelled by steady fire from the new rifles.

For the next five hours the Indians came in waves, but they never breached the American defenses. Six soldiers were killed, including Capt. Powell's second in command. Indian losses were much more severe, Powell claimed: about sixty dead and more than one hundred wounded. In this case, the army estimates do not appear to be exaggerated. Red Cloud had seen the future, and it was shaped by a Springfield Allin rifle.

To the Americans, these simultaneous attacks on two forts ninety miles apart solidified Red Cloud's reputation as the leader of a hostile force to be reckoned with. That his imposing personality had held together a large intertribal alliance for over two seasons of hard fighting was literally awe-inspiring, and his influence showed no signs of letting up. His overall leadership, his organizing genius, and his ability to persuade contentious tribes to band together and direct their hatred against the whites had enabled perhaps the most impressive campaign in the chronicles of Indian warfare.

After the events of early August, one general ominously informed the War Department that he would need 20,000 soldiers to defeat Red Cloud's forces. This perceived siege of the mighty United States of America was what forced the country to the negotiating table.

The first discussions took place in October 1867, when Capt. George Dandy held a meeting with representatives from the Lakota, Arapaho, and Cheyenne. These subchiefs conveyed Red Cloud's insistence that the Bozeman Trail be closed forever and the three forts built along it abandoned; he would not even consider peace without this. The army was staggered by Red Cloud's boldness. But in Washington, the Reconstruction of the South and the protection and completion of the Union Pacific Railroad were deemed higher priorities than control of the Powder River Country.

It was not until April 1868 that another peace commission arrived at Fort Laramie. Red Cloud would not legitimize the council by his presence and instead sent a message reiterating his original demand: begone. A month later, the concessions were agreed to and the Americans ordered the Bozeman Trail closed to all emigrants and miners, and issued a proclamation to abandon "the military posts of C. F. Smith, Phil Kearny and Reno, on what is known as the Powder River route."

Red Cloud waited. He had heard too many white

promises in his life. This time he intended to see the results before signing anything.

The contents of Fort C. F. Smith were sold, and anything that could be hauled from the two lower outposts was loaded onto wagons bound for Fort Laramie. In the final weeks of August 1868, the last wagons rolled out of Reno Station and Fort Phil Kearny. An eerie silence fell over the little plateau between the two Piney Creeks, broken the following dawn when Red Cloud led his warriors down from the hills and burned the fort to the ground. He burned Reno Station the next day.

On November 6, 1868—after making the increasingly nervous white commissioners and army officers wait until the conclusion of the autumn buffalo hunt—the forty-seven-year-old Bad Face warrior chief rode into Fort Laramie and triumphantly signed the treaty whereby the United States conceded to Red Cloud and his people the territory from the Bighorns eastward to the Missouri River, and from the forty-sixth parallel south to the Dakota-Nebraska boundary.

It was understood, at least by the whites, that the Indians would live in the eastern section and reserve the western section, the Powder River Country, as hunting grounds open to all tribes and bands. In the center of this tract, like a glittering jewel, lay the Black Hills. *Paha Sapa.* The Heart of Everything That Is.

It was the proudest moment of Red Cloud's life. That sentiment lasted a mere twelve months, for the Lakota were not finished dying.

One of the seventeen articles in the treaty contained

a vague clause requiring the disparate tribes to live, and remain, on specified pieces of land anchored by Bureau of Indian Affairs trading posts. Red Cloud quite naturally interpreted this as referring to the entire Powder River Country, the Black Hills, and the western swath of present-day South Dakota for which he had just fought, and won, a war.

General Philip Sheridan saw it differently, and began to formulate a long-range plan that would force the Indians, particularly the Lakota, onto reservations well east of the Powder River Country. This would serve the dual purpose of keeping the enemy under observation and gradually making them more reliant on government goods and services. Whereas Red Cloud was thinking of weapons, Gen. Sheridan was thinking of plows.

As part of his strategy, Gen. Sheridan closed Fort Laramie to Indian trading. The Lakota were told that if they wished to trade, they were free to do business at Fort Randall on the Missouri River in distant southeast South Dakota, about as far from *Paha Sapa* as one can travel and still be in the state. To salt the wound, Gen. Sheridan placed none other than the retired general Harney, the hated officer who had staked out the road through the middle of the Powder River Country thirteen years earlier, in charge of the post. Red Cloud was insulted and said that he and his people would have nothing to do with the vicious old "Mad Bear."

With their trading post closed, the Indians had no choice but to relocate to Fort Randall. But Red Cloud and his followers resisted all government efforts to move them closer to the Missouri.

Even after Red Cloud's victories, some docile Lakota, known as "Laramie Loafers," continued to wait for food delivered by U.S. Army supply wagons. *Courtesy American Heritage Center, University of Wyoming*

Though Red Cloud stopped short of declaring war, he could not contain his more militant braves. Skirmishes between army units and Sioux and Cheyenne warriors broke out, particularly on Sitting Bull's Hunkpapa lands on the Upper Missouri and in the Republican River Basin to the south of the Oregon Trail. And though Red Cloud does not seem to have taken an active part in the fights, at one point he sent word to the whites that if they refused to reopen Fort Laramie as an Indian trading post, it should be closed altogether, just as the army had abandoned the Upper Powder forts.

When the army ignored this veiled threat, Red Cloud appeared unexpectedly one morning in March 1869 before Fort Laramie's gates at the head of 1,000 mounted warriors. It was a political show. Instead of attacking, his party slowly rode off to hunt in the Wind River country. He did, however, leave behind lobbyists, in the form of mixed-blood traders, to argue his cause.

The generals running the U.S. Army could be as headstrong as any Indian warrior chief. When Red Cloud, ever the politician, recognized this, instead of starting a new war he decided to take his arguments directly to the top.

To Washington, D.C.

In June 1870, Red Cloud and Spotted Tail accepted a long-standing invitation to visit Washington, D.C., and traveled east at the head of a delegation of Oglalas and Brules. There they were given tours of the Capitol and army and navy facilities, with special emphasis on the War Department's arsenal, where huge coastal cannons and howitzers were stored. For the first time, Red Cloud saw the true military might of the United States.

Ulysses S. Grant, who had been elected president two years earlier, gave a reception for him and the others at the White House. There and in subsequent meetings with government officials, the provisions of the treaty were debated, with the plainspoken Red Cloud acting as lead negotiator. "As a consequence," wrote R. Eli Paul, editor of Red Cloud's memoirs, "he became stunningly famous. The head-warrior-turned-statesman and his entourage took the country by storm. Newspapers recounted his every word and deed, and

One of several delegations that Red Cloud (center) led to
Washington, D.C., between 1870 and the 1890s, where he
met with U.S. government officials, including President Grant,
to advocate on behalf of the Sioux. From left to right:
Red Dog, Little Wound, John Bridgeman (interpreter),
Red Cloud, American Horse, and Red Shirt, 1880.
Courtesy American Heritage Center, University of Wyoming

large crowds of onlookers gathered at every public sighting of the celebrated group."

It was during this journey that Red Cloud ultimately realized the pointlessness of his aspirations. Though he managed to wrangle minor concessions from the government—a new trading post forty miles north of Fort Laramie was promised, for instance—and he may have considered himself the equal of any white man he encountered on his trip east, he had finally recognized the limitations of the Lakota nation as an entity. As he told Secretary of the Interior Jacob D. Cox, "Now we are melting like snow on the hillside, while you are growing like spring grass."

The beginning of the end for Red Cloud's Lakota, and all Plains Indians, had actually arrived one year earlier, in 1869, when the Union Pacific Railroad was completed across southern Wyoming and northern Utah, with a spur line running north to the western Montana goldfields. With the railroad arrived an army of buffalo hunters, whose deadly accurate rifles would soon wipe the prairie clean and do what no battle commander had ever been able to accomplish—drive the starving, destitute Lakota onto the white man's reservations.

On his return from the trip to Washington, D.C., Red Cloud and his Bad Faces continued to roam the Powder River Country, but the end of their lifestyle was as inevitable as the end of the buffalo. Using the last of his dwindling influence, in early 1872 Red Cloud again traveled to Washington, and persuaded the government to set aside a rolling swath of land along the White River in northwestern Nebraska as a new Red Cloud Agency, the first version of which had briefly

Sport-shooting buffalo from the Kansas-Pacific Railroad.
Illustration published in 1871. *Library of Congress*

been located on the North Platte River. The site was visually breathtaking, a partially wooded tract marked by high bluffs that overlooked a green, rolling prairie veined with streams and creeks. Red Cloud, who had played his last card, moved there that same year. He was fifty-one. From this new home he declared, "I shall not go to war any more with whites."

In 1874, gold was discovered in the Black Hills. That *Paha Sapa* had been guaranteed to the tribes by Red Cloud's treaty was of little consequence to the whites. Extracting the gold became a national priority.

An American military campaign, to be led by the cantankerous, hard-drinking General Sheridan, was already being planned. Sheridan's main target was Sitting Bull, who was amassing his own intertribal force to defend the territory. When Sitting Bull's agitators approached Red Cloud, he stuck to his promise. Like a surgeon who had grown weary of blood, he saw no point in seeing more of it shed. Red Cloud knew that taking action against the United States would lead to a grimly waged campaign that would wear down the Indians day after insufferable day. The white soldiers who saw no evil in exterminating his people regardless of age or gender would never give them rest, and their territory would shrink until they were boxed in and forced to choose annihilation or surrender.

General George Armstrong Custer's blunder into the large Lakota and Northern Cheyenne camp on the Little Bighorn in June 1876—the Indians called it the Battle of the Greasy Grass—was the Sioux's last hurrah. The shocking slaughter of

Custer's entire immediate command intensified the national enthusiasm to eliminate the Northern Plains tribes.

Ironically, what the Indians lacked was a strategist on the order of Red Cloud to follow up their great tactical victory at the Little Bighorn. America struck back hard, and the army's operations continued through the spring of 1877, when even Crazy Horse recognized the pointlessness of the fight and turned himself in to soldiers at the Red Cloud Agency. Four months later, Crazy Horse was bayoneted to death by a guard at the agency while allegedly trying to escape from so-called protective custody. Controversy still surrounds his death.

With Crazy Horse dead and Sitting Bull a fugitive in Canada, what was left of the hostile tribes became resigned to their fate: living on the reservation. Once again, sadly, Red Cloud had been prophetic. In 1878 the Red Cloud Agency, Red Cloud along with it, was relocated to southwest South Dakota and renamed the Pine Ridge Indian Reservation.

American Horse (left) and Red Cloud (right) were now the most famous chiefs in the United States. They posed for this photograph at Pine Ridge in 1891.

Afterword

Few people have the ability to completely move away from their life's philosophy, particularly in old age. Red Cloud was one of them. His attitude toward the reservation, once the symbol of a caged life unworthy of living, altered once he was established at Pine Ridge. He would adhere to the white man's lifestyle, live in a house, wear white men's clothes, engage in white people's commercial activities, and send his children to their schools. He had once been a man of a certain place and time; now he was a man of another place and time.

His political gifts were numerous and ingrained, and he wielded them to remain the physical and spiritual leader of the Oglalas. Red Cloud had not changed, but he had adapted, and unlike Sitting Bull and Crazy Horse and the others who fought on, he had seen his people's future. He understood that he, and they, had been overcome by historical forces.

Over the decades, Red Cloud made several more trips east

Red Cloud (right), his wife, Pretty Owl, and an unidentified man at home in Pine Ridge, 1890. *Photo by W. R. Cross, Library of Congress*

to plead for better conditions for his people, especially the next generation of Lakota. Unlike his military expeditions, his political aims were destined to fail, though not for lack of effort.

In a remarkable address to President Rutherford B. Hayes on September 26, 1877, he complained about the dry, dusty, infertile soil of the Pine Ridge Indian Reservation and declared, "God made this earth for us and everybody; there is good streams, good lands; and I wish you to take me to a good place to raise my children. The place where I am now was selected with the advice of the Great Father. I also want schools to enable my children to read and write so they will be as wise as the white man's children. I have the same feelings as all the white men have for their families; they love their children, as I do mine, and I would like to raise my children well."

As the years passed, Red Cloud remained a respected if increasingly distant figure on the Pine Ridge Indian Reservation. His children had children, and his oldest son, Jack, would succeed him as the tribe's head man.

On July 4, 1903, the eighty-two-year-old Red Cloud, nearly blind, made his final public address to a gathering of Lakota. "My sun is set," he said. "My day is done. Darkness is stealing over me. Before I lie down to rise no more, I will speak to my people. Hear me, my friends, for it is not the time for me to tell you a lie. The Great Spirit made us, the Indians, and gave us this land we live in. He gave us the buffalo, the antelope, and the deer for food and clothing. We moved our hunting grounds from the Minnesota to the Platte and from the Mississippi to the great mountains. No one put bounds on us. We were free as the winds, and like the eagle, heard no man's commands."

The white men had changed all that. They were too numerous and too powerful, and their arrival marked the passing of an era as surely as the disappearance of the buffalo. "Shadows are long and dark before me," Red Cloud concluded. "I shall soon lie down to rise no more. While my spirit is with my body the smoke of my breath shall be towards the Sun, for he knows all things and knows that I am still true to him."

On December 10, 1909, Red Cloud died peacefully in

Red Cloud, age 77, 1898.
Library of Congress

his sleep at the age of eighty-seven. His death prompted headlines around the country. In a lengthy appreciation, the *New York Times* noted, "When Red Cloud fought the whites he did so to the best of his ability. But when he signed the first peace paper he buried his tomahawk and this peace pact was never broken."

It was, of course, broken many times—by the U.S. government.

Red Cloud's grave is in a cemetery atop a hill on the Pine Ridge Indian Reservation, a short walk from the Red Cloud Heritage Center. From there, on a clear day, you can almost see the sacred *Paha Sapa*.

Edward S. Curtis took this photograph of Red Cloud on
December 26, 1905. *Library of Congress*

Acknowledgments

This book would not have been possible without the courtesy and expertise of curators, researchers, historians, and all those others who staff the centers where so much information— some of it proving quite difficult to unearth—was found and generously shared with us. In particular, we are grateful to the American Antiquarian Society and Jackie Penny; American Heritage Center, University of Wyoming, and Rick Ewig, John Waggener, and Hailey Kaylenne Woodall; American Museum of Natural History and Barry Landua, Kristen Mable, and Mai Reitmeyer; Bozeman Trail Association; Center for Western Studies and Elizabeth Thrond; East Hampton Public Library; Eli Ricker Collection; Fort Phil Kearny State Historic Site and Christopher Morton; John Jermain Memorial Library; Library of Congress and Frederick Plummer and Courtney Pruitt; Montana Historical Society and Rebecca Kohl and Zoe Ann Stoltz; Nebraska State Historical Society and Andrea Faling; Smithsonian Institution and Megan Gambino, Daisy Njoku, and Gina Rappaport; South Dakota Historical Society and Patti Edman; South Dakota State Archives and Matthew Reitzel; Western History Association; The Wyoming Room, Sheridan County Public Library, and Judy Slack; and Wyoming State Archives and Cindy Brown.

We want to give a special mention to the eminent historian Robert Utley, who kindly agreed to review a draft of this manuscript for omissions and any errors in both judgment and fact. His remarks and guidance were, and are, greatly appreciated. He made our book better.

Similarly, we send special thank-yous to Mary Anne Red Cloud and the other members of the Red Cloud family, as well as the residents of the Pine Ridge Indian Reservation and the hard-working staffers at the Red Cloud Heritage Center, for their insights and recollections.

From the beginning of this project we received enthusiastic support from Jofie Ferrari-Adler, Jonathan Karp, Sarah Nalle, and everyone at Simon & Schuster. Similarly, Ruta Rimas and Justin Chanda at Margaret K. McElderry Books, and Kate Waters, the adapter, proved invaluable collaborators and we are very grateful to each of them. And however many times we thank Nat Sobel and the crack staff at Sobel-Weber Associates, it is never enough—but here is one more thank-you anyway.

As with any long and involved writing project, this book benefited by the authors having the encouragement and support of family and friends. Our gratitude goes to Denise McDonald and Leslie Reingold; Michael Gambino, David Hughes, and Bobby Kelly; and our children, Brendan Clavin, Kathryn Clavin, and Liam-Antoine DeBusschere-Drury.

Time Line

The dates below are according to the white calendar. Red Cloud and the Sioux did not divide up time in this way. Some geographic names are white names; some are Indian.

May 1821 Red Cloud is born on the banks of the Platte River in the Nebraska Territory

1826 Red Cloud's father dies, and Red Cloud's mother and her children return to the Oglala Sioux band

1841 Red Cloud kills Bull Bear

1849 U.S. government purchases Fort Laramie from the American Fur Company

Around 1850 Red Cloud marries Pretty Owl

September 1851 First treaty of Fort Laramie, the Horse Creek Treaty

Summer 1855 Red Cloud is admitted into the aristocratic class in his first Pipe Dance

August 1857 Council at Bear Butte

April 12, 1861 U.S. Civil War begins

May 20, 1862 Homestead Act passes, resulting in a flood of settlers

Summer 1862 Dakota War in Minnesota

November 29, 1864 Massacre at Sand Creek

April 9, 1865 U.S. Civil War ends

Spring 1865 Lakota and Cheyenne war council

July 1865 Wagon trains begin to cross the Powder River Country on the way to Montana goldfields

Fall 1865 Major General John Pope arrives at Fort Laramie to secure the Bozeman Trail

1866–November 6, 1868 The group of skirmishes, ambushes and attacks that became known as Red Cloud's War

June 5–18, 1866 Unsuccessful peace conference at Fort Laramie

June 13, 1866 Colonel Carrington arrives at Fort Laramie

July 7, 1866 Fort Phil Kearny construction begins

December 21, 1866 Battle of the Hundred in the Hands, aka the Fetterman massacre

August 1868 Red Cloud burns Fort Reno and Fort Phil Kearny to the ground

November 6, 1868 Red Cloud signs the Second Treaty of Fort Laramie

1869 Union Pacific Railroad is complete, cutting through the *Paha Sapa,* the sacred Black Hills

June 1870 Red Cloud's first visit to Washington, D.C., to negotiate with President Grant

1872 Red Cloud Agency is set up

July 2, 1874 Geologists traveling with Lieutenant Colonel George Armstrong Custer on an exploratory expedition into the *Paha Sapa,* the Black Hills, find evidence of gold

1875 Red Cloud again travels to Washington to meet with President Grant

June 25, 1876 Battle of the Greasy Grass, aka Battle of the Little Bighorn

September 26, 1877 Red Cloud gives a famous speech to President Rutherford B. Hayes

1878 Red Cloud Agency is moved and renamed Pine Ridge Indian Reservation

1881 Red Cloud steps down as war chief of the Lakota

December 10, 1909 Red Cloud dies at the Pine Ridge Indian Reservation in South Dakota at the age of 88

Glossary

LAKOTA WORDS AND PHRASES

akicita a select male society of warriors and marshals; also, individual members of this group

blotahunka ataya head of the *akicita*

catku the section of a Sioux tepee reserved for and used by the head of the family

hunka a Lakota ceremony of inclusion or adoption

Ite Sica Bad Faces

Mato Paha Bear Butte

mini wakan whiskey

Paha Sapa Black Hills

Wakan Tanka the universe; also, the Supreme Being

wakpamni distribution of goods by the U.S. government to the Indians

wicasa wakan vision seeker

GEOGRAPHIC TERMS

basin (river basin) an area of land drained by rivers and streams

bluff a cliff or a mountain with a very steep face or sides

butte an isolated hill or mountain with steep sides; a butte has a smaller top than a mesa

coulee a small stream or a dry streambed; also called a gully

draw the low area between two high ridges

floodplain the area next to a river that floods when the river is high

mesa a large hill with steep sides and a flat top

pass a low place on a mountain range through which one can travel

plains large, flat areas of land

plateau an area of level ground that is higher than the surrounding area

prairie a large area of flat or rolling land with grass but few trees

ravine a steep, extremely narrow valley

ridgeline the line following or marking a ridgetop

snowmelt runoff produced by melting snow

MILITARY TERMS

adjutant a military officer who is the assistant to a more senior officer

agency an administrative division (for instance, of the government)

bastion a part of a fortification from which cannon shoot

blockhouse a military building made of heavy logs with slits to accommodate guns; often the second story is wider than the first

catwalk a narrow walkway at the top of a building or at the side of a bridge

duty roster a list of tasks soldiers are assigned to

field gun a gun to be used in everyday fighting

fletching the arrangement of feathers on an arrow

form up to gather in an orderly arrangement

grapeshot a cluster of small iron balls shot from a cannon

howitzer a short cannon

picket a group of people serving as guards, also called sentries

prime [a musket] to prepare for firing by inserting a cartridge

remuda a herd of horses usually gathered to be used on a daily basis

skirmish a minor fight

stockade a line of strong posts set away from a fort to create a wall or fence

tack articles uses on horses such as saddle and bridle

volley simultaneous discharge of a number of weapons

GENERAL TERMS

amphitheater a flat area surrounded by slopes or, if a building, a room with seating rising up from the floor

bell mare a female horse or mule that wears a bell and serves as the leader of the herd

chips (buffalo) dried dung that can be used as fuel

concentric having the same center; concentric circles have the same center but each circle is larger going out from the center

devilment mischief

drove (buffalo) a large number

emigrant one who leaves one place to travel to live in another place

feint to make a pretend movement, especially in a fight

fisheries streams, rivers, and oceans where fish are abundant

gypsum a mineral

hardtack a hard biscuit, bread, or cracker that does not spoil easily

hobble to fasten together legs to keep animals from straying

monogamous being married to one person at a time

parley to discuss terms with an enemy; to discuss

pasturage pasture or land where plants grow that animals can eat

pemmican a long-lasting food made of pounded dried meat mixed with animal fat

pommel the knob at the front of a saddle; also, the knob at the hilt of a sword

quirt a riding whip (noun); to whip (verb)

quiver a case for carrying arrows

Reconstruction the plan to unify the country and fix the economy after the Civil War

retaliate to get revenge, to repay in kind

scamp a rascal

scat animal excrement

serape a shawl worn over the shoulders especially by men

stock livestock, such as oxen and mules

sutler a civilian shop owner at an army post

teamsters someone who drives a team of animals usually pulling a wagon

thicket a dense area of shrubs or small trees

travois a vehicle pulled by a horse or mule consisting of two poles supporting a platform on which to carry belongings

wheelwright someone who makes and repairs wheel and wheeled vehicles

whiteout a condition in a snowy area when nothing casts a shadow, no horizon is visible, and only dark objects are visible

Places to Visit

The Heritage Center
Red Cloud Indian School,
Pine Ridge Indian Reservation, South Dakota
http://www.redcloudschool.org/museum/
Cited as one of the top ten places to honor American Indian life, this museum has an extensive collection of historical Lakota art.

Sioux Indian Museum
Rapid City, South Dakota
https://www.doi.gov/iacb/our-museums/sioux/
The museum exhibits historical clothing, weapons, household items, horse tack, and children's toys as well as examples of contemporary Sioux art.

Akta Lakota Museum & Cultural Center
Chamberlain, South Dakota
http://www.stjo.org/
Associated with St. Joseph's Indian School, the museum celebrates Lakota culture with art, artifacts, and cultural programs.

Crazy Horse Memorial
Custer, South Dakota
https://crazyhorsememorial.org/
The Crazy Horse Memorial is located in the Black Hills of South Dakota near the town of Custer. It is an enormous mountain sculpture carved by Korczak Ziolkowski, who was an assistant sculptor on the Mount Rushmore presidential carvings. He worked on the memorial from 1948 until his death in 1982. At the welcome center, you can also visit the Native American Educational & Cultural Center and the Indian Museum of North America.

Tatanka: Story of the Bison
Deadwood, South Dakota
http://www.storyofthebison.com/
Kevin Costner's museum is a tribute to the buffalo, with sculpture and an interpretive center.

National Museum of the American Indian/
Smithsonian Institution
Washington, D.C., and New York, New York
http://www.nmai.si.edu/
With extensive exhibits and programming, this museum celebrates Native cultures from Hawaii to Maine. Some exhibits travel.

High Plains Western Heritage Center
Spearfish, South Dakota
http://www.westernheritagecenter.com/
Primarily commemorating settlement of the area by whites, the museum chronicles the rise in ranching and mining in North Dakota, South Dakota, Nebraska, Montana, and Wyoming.

For More Information

TO READ: BOOKS

Bial, Raymond. *The Sioux*. New York: Benchmark Books, 1999.

Bruchac, Joseph. *Thirteen Moons on Turtle's Back: A Native American Year of Moons*. New York: Philomel Books, 1992. Celebrates the seasons of the year with poems based on legends from the Sioux, Cherokee, and Cree.

Goble, Paul. *Red Cloud's War: Brave Eagle's Account of the Fetterman Fight, 21 December 1866*. Bloomington, IN: Wisdom Tales, 2015. Excerpts from a first-person account, beautifully illustrated in an Indian style.

Hyslop, Stephen G. *The Old West*. Washington, D.C.: National Geographic Society, 2015. Although the text is written for adults, the photographs in this book bring the era to life. Concentration is on white settlers.

Paul, R. Eli, editor. *The Autobiography of Red Cloud: Warrior Leader of the Oglalas*. Helena, MT: Montana Historical Society, 1997.

Spinner, Stephanie. *Who Was Sitting Bull?* New York: Grosset & Dunlap, 2014.

Viegas, Jennifer. *The Fort Laramie Treaty, 1868: A Primary Source Examination of the Treaty That Established a Sioux Reservation in the Black Hills of Dakota.* New York: Rosen, 2006.

Winner, Cherie. *Bison.* New York: Cooper Square Publishing, 2001.

Zimmerman, Dwight Jon. *Saga of the Sioux.* New York: Henry Holt, 2011. An adaptation for young readers of Dee Brown's *Bury My Heart at Wounded Knee.*

TO READ: WEB PAGES

http://www.pbs.org/weta/thewest/people/i_r/redcloud.htm One page from the extensive and wonderful PBS series *The West,* with links to events by date and to places such as Fort Laramie and Fort Phil Kearny.

http://www.pbs.org/wgbh/americanexperience/features /biography/grant-redcloud/ Biography of Red Cloud and his interactions with President Grant from the PBS series *American Experience.*

http://www.wyohistory.org/encyclopedia/brief-history -bozeman-trail/ A history of the Bozeman Trail, with photographs, maps, and settlers' sketches.

TO WATCH

https://www.youtube.com/watch?v=9M9-5Twz0q8 "The American West 05: Gold in the Black Hills" Excellent video of the discovery of gold and its effects on the Sioux, using the 1874 diaries of a settler, Annie Talent. (9 minutes 16 seconds)

https://www.youtube.com/watch?v=fBGiHFoJVYI A photo
slideshow of images of Red Cloud, with a traditional
Lakota Sioux chant in the background. (3 minutes 36
seconds)

Extended bibliography and notes can be found in the original
edition of this book.

A Note on the Cover Art and Artist

Donald F. Montileaux (Yellowbird) is a modern-day storyteller,
rekindling the images of the Lakota lifestyle by painting the
people as they were. He created the art for the cover of this
book and is an enrolled member of the Oglala Lakota Tribe.
Montileaux regards himself as having a mission: "To portray the
Lakota, the Native Americans, in an honest way. To illustrate
them as people who hunted buffalo, made love, raised children,
cooked meals, and lived."

His artwork is often painted on accounting books and journals, or ledgers. During the transition from being a nomadic
people on the plains to confinement on reservations, the Lakota
people bartered with Indian Agents, traders, and military officers
for their ledgers, which were filled with entries and no longer
useable other than as a bartering item to the Native American.
The Lakota's transition from painting on hides to drawing on
the pages from these books reflected their traditional lifestyles,
and the stories told and retold through the generations.

These ledger drawings are a way of preserving the simplistic
style of art by Montileaux's ancestors. He prefers to work on
ledger paper dating from 1870 to 1940. Ledger art had a revi-
talized interest in the 1980s and has gained in popularity since.

Index